ITALIAN DESSERTS

Anthony Parkinson

"Italian Desserts"

TABLE OF CONTENTS

Cakes, Pastries, Tarts, Torte and Sweet Breads 1

Cookies 65

Fried Desserts 94

Puddings and Creams 142

Cakes, Pastries, Tarts, Torte and Sweet Breads

Apricot-Fig Crostatas

Purchased jam provides a short cut for this recipe or you can make your own by reconstituting 18 chopped, dried figs in boiling water. Simply cook until figs soften and water is reduced by half. Add 1/4 cup sugar and continue to cook until soft and jammy.

One 17.3-ounce box (2 sheets) frozen puff pastry, thawed

1/2 cup apricot preserves
1/4 teaspoon ground cinnamon

8 tablespoons fig jam
12 small apricots (about 1 1/4 pounds total), halved, pitted

2 teaspoons turbinado sugar

Preheat oven to 400 degrees F. Cut each pastry sheet into two 5 3/4-inch rounds. Transfer pastry rounds to baking sheets. Pierce pastry rounds with fork, leaving 1-inch border of each pastry unpierced. Chill 1 hour.

Blend apricot preserves in processor until smooth. Stir preserves and cinnamon in heavy small saucepan over medium heat until warm.

Spread 2 tablespoons fig jam in center of each pastry, leaving 1-inch border. Place 6 apricot halves cut side down on jam atop each pastry. Brush with warm preserve mixture. Fold borders in to form 1/2-inch edge; crimp as needed. Bake 10 minutes. Reduce oven temperature to 350 degrees F. Bake until pastry is golden and apricots are glazed, about 20 minutes longer. Cool on cooling rack, about 20 minutes.

Sprinkle turbinado sugar equally over each and serve immediately.

Bonet Recipe

A traditional dessert from Piedmont, this one is made in the Langhe with cream from the top of the milk, while in other areas of the region whole milk is used. Both produce equally good results, but the second (this recipe) is a little lighter.

3 egg yolks
1/2 cups sugar
1 cup amaretti cookies, crushed
1 tablespoon unsweetened cocoa powder
2 cups milk
1 tablespoon rum
3 egg whites, stiffly beaten

Preheat the oven to 300 degrees F. Beat the egg yolks with the sugar until smooth. In a food processor, combine the egg yolk mixture with the amaretti, cocoa, milk and rum. Process for a couple of minutes until very well mixed. Strain the mixture into a bowl. Gently fold in the egg whites. Pour into four 2 in individual molds or a single large 10 in ring-mold.

Set the mold(s) in a roasting pan and add hot water to reach halfway up the sides of the molds. Bake in the oven for about 30 minutes, or until set. Let cool. Turn out onto a plate and serve.

Blueberry Ricotta Squares

A blueberry coffeecake with a ricotta cheese topping. Original recipe yield: 1 - 9 inch square dish.

1 cup all-purpose flour
3/4 cup white sugar
1 1/4 teaspoons baking powder
1/3 cup milk
1/4 cup shortening
1 egg
1/2 teaspoon lemon extract
1 1/2 cups blueberries
2 eggs, beaten
1 1/4 cups ricotta cheese
1/3 cup white sugar
1/4 teaspoon vanilla extract

Preheat the oven to 350 degrees F (175 degrees C). Grease a 9 inch square baking dish.

In a large bowl, stir together the flour, 3/4 cup of sugar, and baking powder. Add the milk, shortening, 1 egg, and lemon extract, and use an electric mixer to mix on low speed for 1 minute, then on medium speed for 1 minute. Pour the batter into the prepared pan, and spread evenly. Sprinkle blueberries over the batter.

In a medium bowl, stir together 2 beaten eggs, ricotta cheese, 1/3 cup of sugar, and vanilla extract. Spoon this mixture over the blueberries, and spread evenly.

4

Bake for 55 to 60 minutes in the preheated oven, until a knife inserted near the center comes out clean. Cool completely before cutting into squares and serving.

Bourbon Chocolate Cake

This is my most-requested cake recipe. Not only is it delicious, but you don't need a mixer to make it -just whisk all the ingredients together.

2 cups all-purpose flour
1 teaspoon baking soda
Pinch of salt
1 3/4 cups hot coffee
1/4 cup bourbon
5 ounces unsweetened baking chocolate, cut into small pieces
2 sticks (8 ounces) unsalted butter, cut into small pieces
2 cups sugar
2 eggs, at room temperature
1 teaspoon vanilla extract

Preheat the oven to 275 degrees F. Grease and flour two 8- or 9-inch round pans. Sift together the flour, baking soda, and salt.

Combine the coffee, bourbon, chocolate, and butter in a large covered metal bowl. Let stand until completely melted, then whisk together. Whisk in the sugar and cool. Whisk in the flour mixture in 2 batches, then the eggs and the vanilla. Pour the batter into the prepared pans and bake for 45 minutes (checking after 30 minutes for even baking) or until a toothpick inserted in the center comes out clean. Cool the cakes completely in the pans on wire racks. You can then either refrigerate them in the pans, wrapped in plastic, or use them right away, though it's easier to decorate a cool cake. To remove the cakes from the pans, run a knife around the inside edges of the pan and place it over a low flame to melt the grease, making sure to keep the pan moving to prevent burning. The cake should slide out easily when you invert the pan.

Cannoli with Ricotta Cream with Bittersweet Chocolate and Almonds

Tip: This ricotta cream filling for cannoli has bits of almond paste, chocolate and toasted almonds for incredible texture and flavor.

Other necessary recipes: Cannoli Shells
One 8.8-ounce package almond paste
1 1/2 15-ounce containers whole-milk ricotta cheese

1 1/2 cups chilled whipping cream
3 tablespoons Amaretto liqueur
3 tablespoons confectioners' sugar
1 1/4 teaspoons ground cinnamon
10 ounces bittersweet chocolate, chopped
1 1/4 cups sliced almonds, toasted

Blend almond paste in food processor until coarse crumbs form. Transfer almond crumbs to large bowl. Add ricotta cheese; stir to blend.

Combine cream, Amaretto, confectioners' sugar and cinnamon in another large bowl. Using electric mixer, beat cream mixture until firm peaks form. Fold whipped cream into ricotta mixture. Fold in chopped chocolate and toasted sliced almonds. (Mixture can be prepared 1 day ahead. Cover and refrigerate.)

Spoon cream mixture into pastry bag. Just before serving, pipe filling into cannoli shells.

Chestnut Cake

There are chestnut forests in many regions of Italy, and this autumn fruit provides the raw material for sweet confections that have passed into international cuisine. Montebianco, for example, is a delicious treat made with boiled chestnuts put through a sieve and mixed with whipped cream. This castagnaccio, however, is made only in Tuscany, and is an example of the old unleavened cakes known as stiacciate, among the earliest foods consumed by humans. The castagnaccio is served in slices as a dessert or sometimes is cut into small squares and eaten at the end of the meal.

2 cups water
3 1/4 cups chestnut flour
Salt
1/4 cup extra-virgin olive oil
2 tablespoons golden raisins
2 tablespoons small thin strips of orange zest
1/4 cup walnut pieces
1/4 cup pine nuts
1 tablespoon rosemary leaves

Preheat the oven to 400 degrees F. Whisk the water into the chestnut flour until smooth and without lumps. The mixture should be fairly liquid. Add a pinch of salt, olive oil, golden raisins, orange zest and walnuts, Mix thoroughly.

Pour the batter into a round cake pan about 14-16 in in diameter. Sprinkle the surface with a little oil and scatter the pine nuts and rosemary leaves on top.

Bake in the oven for 35 to 40 minutes, or until the surface is covered by a dark crunchy crust. Serve cold, molded or unmolded.

Chocolate Hazelnut Cake with Pear Compote

Chocolate, pears and hazelnuts are definitely an unbeatable combination in a dessert, and this cake is no exception. This light, subtly sweet cake is created with chopped pears for flavor and added moisture, and is served with tasty pear compote and a dollop of whipped cream.

Cake

1 cup hazelnuts
1 cup icing sugar
2/3 cup flour
2 tablespoons cocoa powder
2 1/2 teaspoons baking powder
pinch of cinnamon
1/2 cup unsalted butter
2 large eggs plus 1 egg yolk
2 teaspoons vanilla
1 ripe pear, peeled, and cut into 1/2 dice
1/2 cup mini chocolate chips

Pear Compote

4 ripe pears, peeled and cut into 1/2 inch dice
1/2 cups chopped hazelnuts
1/2 cup white wine
4 tablespoons butter
4 tablespoons sugar
1/2 teaspoon cinnamon

Topping
(8oz) container whipping cream
1/2 cup powdered sugar

For the cake, preheat the oven to 325 degrees F. Spread the nuts out on a baking sheet and toast for about 10 minutes or until they begin to change color. Place the warm nuts in a kitchen towel and rub, to remove as much of the skins as possible. Raise the oven temperature to 375 degrees F.

Place the nuts in a food processor and grind finely. Butter and flour a 9" cake pan. In a bowl, mix together the nuts, flour, cocoa, baking powder and cinnamon. In a separate bowl beat the butter and sugar until fluffy. Add the eggs, extra yolk and vanilla, beating after each addition. Add the dry ingredients and mix well. Fold in the chopped pear and chocolate chips. Bake for about 30 minutes or until a knife comes out clean. Cool.

To prepare the compote, put all the ingredients except the nuts in a pan and cook until the pears are tender and the mixture is thickened. Fold in the chopped nuts. Whip the heavy cream until thick peaks form, adding the sugar towards the end.

To serve, place a slice of cake on a plate, spoon a little of the compote over it, and add a dollop of whip cream.

Chocolate-Hazelnut Torte

Candies, ice cream and tortes throughout Italy are flavored with gianduja, the pleasing combination of hazelnuts and chocolate; those with the richest taste and most intense aroma come from Piedmont. This torte is typical of ones served in the charming Piedmontese town of Alba.

1 1/2 cups hazelnuts
1 cup confectioners' sugar
3 tablespoons potato starch (potato flour)
2/3 cup unbleached all-purpose flour
1 1/2 tablespoons unsweetened cocoa
2 1/2 teaspoons baking powder
Pinch of ground cinnamon
1/2 cup unsalted butter, cut into small pieces
2 extra-large eggs, lightly beaten, plus 1 extra-large egg yolk
2 teaspoons vanilla extract

Preheat an oven to 325 degrees F. Spread the hazelnuts in a single layer on a baking sheet and toast in the oven until they just begin to change color and the skins begin to loosen, 8-10 minutes. Spread the warm nuts on a kitchen towel. Cover with another kitchen towel and rub against the nuts to remove as much of the skins as possible. Let cool.

Raise the oven temperature to 450 degrees F. Butter and flour a cake pan 9 inches in diameter.

In a food processor fitted with the metal blade or in a blender, combine 1/2 cup of the peeled, cooled hazelnuts and the confectioners' sugar. Process just until the hazelnuts are finely ground, almost to a flour. (Do not over process.)

In a bowl, combine the ground nut mixture, the potato starch, all-purpose flour, cocoa, baking powder and cinnamon. Using an electric mixer set on medium speed, beat for a few seconds to aerate the flour mixture. Add the butter and continue to beat until the butter is in very small pieces. Beat in the whole eggs and the egg yolk and the vanilla until blended. Increase the speed to   *11* medium-high and beat until the mixture is fluffy and a light cocoa color, 2-3 minutes.

Pour the batter into the prepared pan and level the surface. Place in the center of the oven and immediately reduce the heat to 400 degrees F. Bake until a knife inserted in the center comes out clean, 30-35 minutes.

While the cake is baking, place the remaining 1 cup hazelnuts in the food processor fitted with the metal blade or the blender. Process just until the hazelnuts are coarsely ground.

When the cake is done, transfer it to a rack; let cool for 5 minutes. Run a sharp knife around the edge of the pan to loosen the cake sides and invert onto the rack. Then place, right side up, on a serving plate. Immediately sprinkle the ground hazelnuts evenly over the top and press lightly to adhere. Let cool completely and serve.

Chocolate Hazelnut Truffle Tart

Decorating options are many. Either create a lattice effect with sieved cocoa butter and whole hazelnuts or zig zags of white and/or milk chocolate or completely cover the top with chocolate curls or shavings. This is a wonderful do-ahead dessert in that it can be made 2-3 days ahead.

Tip: When making such a decadent dessert uses only the best ingredients. Scharffen Berger bittersweet chocolate rivals the finest European chocolate with its distinctive fruity taste and multiple layers of flavors. It is excellent for baking, making candies and truffles, and for eating on its own.

For Crust
2 1/2 ounces toasted, husked hazelnuts
3/4 cup of all-purpose flour
1/4 cup packed golden brown sugar
6 tablespoons (3/4 stick) unsalted butter, chilled, cut up into pieces
1 1/2 teaspoons vanilla extract

For Filling
1 1/4 cups heavy cream
3 tablespoons unsalted bitter
12 ounces imported bittersweet chocolate, chopped
3 tablespoons Frangelico liqueur
Whole hazelnuts, chocolate or cocoa powder, for garnish

FOR CRUST: Preheat oven to 350 degrees F. Finely grind nuts in food processor (2/3 cup). Add flour and sugar. Pulse to combine. Distribute butter over flour mixture. Pulse until coarse meal forms, about 8 pulses. Add vanilla and pulse until moist clumps form, about 12 long pulses. Gather dough into ball and flatten.

Press dough into 11-inch tart pan with removable bottom to form 1/4-inch-thick crust. Refrigerate 30 minutes. Line with foil and pie weights. Bake until dough is set about 15 minutes. Remove foil and pie weights. Bake until dry and cooked through, about 10 minutes. Cool completely. *13*

FOR FILLING: Place cream and butter in medium saucepan. Bring to simmer over medium heat. Remove from heat. Add chocolate and whisk until smooth. Let cool 15 minutes. Stir in Frangelico. Pour into prepared crust. Chill overnight. Cover when set.

Sift over cocoa powder and garnish with 12 whole hazelnuts.

Ciambellone

This is a traditional Easter Bread recipe that is a cross between a cake and sweet bread.

8 cups flour
6 eggs
2 teaspoons vanilla
2 cups of sugar
2 cups of milk
2 teaspoons cinnamon
1 cup crisco oil
2 teaspoons baking powder
zest from 1 1/2 lemons, finely chopped

Garnish

Milk
Granulated Sugar
Colored Sprinkles

Make a mound with 6 cups of the flour on a board or the counter, creating a well in the center. Using a fork or your fingers, begin alternating the liquid and other dry ingredients into the well, mixing into the flour at the sides. Continue to mix until all the ingredients are combined, adding additional flour as needed to make workable dough. Begin to knead the dough and continue until it is smooth. Divide into 4 equal parts and shape into coils. Brush the tops lightly with the milk, and sprinkle on both the sugar and the sprinkles. Bake at 350 degree F. oven for about 40 minutes or until golden in color.

Custard Pie

Pastry Dough

2 cups flour
1/3 cup sugar
Pinch of salt
1/2 tsp. baking powder
8 tablespoons butter
2 eggs, beaten

Pastry Cream

4 egg yolks
2/3 cup sugar, divided
1/2 cup flour
2 cups milk
2 tsp. grated orange zest
2 tsp. vanilla extract
1 cup cherry jam

For dough

In a bowl, combine flour, sugar, salt, and baking powder.
Using a pastry blender or fork, cut the butter into the dry
ingredients. Stir in eggs.

Transfer the mixture to a floured surface and knead just to form a
dough.

Press into a disk, wrap in plastic wrap and refrigerate 1 hour.

For cream

In a bowl, beat yolks until light and creamy. Beat in 1/3 cup
sugar. Sift in flour and stir until smooth.

In a saucepan, bring milk, zest, and 1/3 cup sugar to a boil.
Whisk a third of the milk into the eggs then whisk the eggs back
into the milk .

Continue cooking and whisking over medium-low heat until the mixture thickens, about 2 minutes.

Remove from heat and add vanilla. Pour into a bowl, cover and refrigerate until cold.

To assemble pie

Preheat oven to 350 degrees F. Butter a 9-inch round cake pan. Divide the dough in half and roll one piece into a round that will cover the bottom and sides of the pan.

Place dough in pan and trim even with top of pan.

Spoon in half of pastry cream. Spread jam over cream and cover with remaining cream.

Roll remaining dough into a 9-inch circle and place on top of pie. To seal, use a small knife to tuck the top crust into the pan around the edge.

Bake 45 minutes or until brown. Allow to cool in pan before removing. Refrigerate 1 hour before serving.

Fresh Peach Tart

Pasta frolla, the classic Italian pastry dough, may also be made
with butter for a flakier crust: use 3/4 cup chilled unsalted butter,
cut into pieces, for the oil, only 1 egg and omit the vinegar.

For Filling

3 1/2 lb ripe yet firm yellow peaches, peeled, pitted and chopped
1/2 cup sugar or 1/3 cup honey, or to taste
1/2 cup dry Italian white wine

For Pastry

1/4 cup slivered blanched almonds
1/2 cup sugar
2 cups all-purpose flour
Pinch of baking soda
Pinch of salt
2 extra-large eggs
2 teaspoons vanilla extract
3/4 teaspoon minced lemon zest
3/4 teaspoon minced orange zest
1/3 cup mild flavored extra-virgin olive oil
1 teaspoon distilled white vinegar

FOR FILLING: In a bowl, toss together the peaches and sugar or
honey; let stand for 1 hour. Then, in a saucepan, combine the
peaches and wine. Bring to a boil; reduce the heat to low and
simmer, uncovered, until soft, 60-70 minutes. Drain and let cool.

FOR PASTRY: In a food processor fitted with the metal blade or
in a blender, combine the almonds and a little bit of the sugar.
Process until finely ground. If using a blender, pour the nut
mixture into the bowl of an electric mixer. To the processor or
mixer, add the remaining sugar, the flour, baking soda and salt.
Pulse or beat briefly until blended.

In a small bowl, whisk together the eggs, vanilla and lemon and orange zests; set aside. Turn the processor on or set the mixer on low speed (using a paddle attachment if you have one) and pour in the oil, then the vinegar, and finally the egg mixture, mixing for only a few seconds until a ball of dough forms. Divide into 2 portions, one twice as large as the other. Cover and refrigerate the smaller portion.

Preheat an oven to 425 degrees F. Place the larger dough portion between 2 sheets of flour-dusted waxed paper. Roll into a round about 11 inches in diameter and 1/8 inch thick. Peel off one piece of paper and transfer the round, paper side up, to a tart pan with a removable bottom 9 inches in diameter and 1 1/4 inches deep. Remove the remaining paper and press the pastry into the pan; trim off the overhang. Spread the filling over the pastry.

Roll out the remaining dough portion in the same manner, forming a round 9 inches in diameter. Using a fluted or plain pastry wheel, cut into strips 1/2 inch wide. Using longer strips near the center, place half of the strips about 1/2 inch apart on top of the pie. Place the remaining strips at a right angle to the first strips, forming a lattice; trim off any overhang. Press the strips against the rim to seal securely.

Place on a baking sheet and put in the center of the oven. Reduce the heat to 375 degrees F and bake for 25-30 minutes. Rotate the tart to ensure even browning and reduce the heat to 300 degrees. Continue to bake until the crust is golden and the filling puffs slightly, 20-25 minutes longer. Let cool before serving.

Holiday Cheesecake

This is a great cheesecake for the holidays as it incorporates ingredients associated with eggnog such as eggs, nutmeg, and rum. In this cheesecake, I added a cranberry topping which made a very attractive presentation. By slow cooking this cheesecake in a water bath, you avoid any cracking and the cheesecake remains very light and creamy. To garnish my cheesecake as shown, I rolled fresh cranberries first in lightly beaten egg white, and then in extra fine sugar. I then placed them in the refrigerator to set. I decorated my cake plate with fresh greens, and added the sugared cranberries.

For Crust
9 graham crackers (use cinnamon graham if desired)
2 tablespoons sugar
1 1/2 teaspoons cinnamon (if using regular graham crackers)
1/4 – 1/3 cup unsalted butter, melted
1/2 cup finely chopped pecans

For Filling
1 1/2 pounds cream cheese at room temperature
3/4 cup sugar
4 tablespoons rum
1 teaspoon vanilla extract
3/4 teaspoon ground nutmeg
3 large eggs at room temperature

Baked Topping
1 1/2 cups sour cream
2 tablespoons sugar
1/2 teaspoon vanilla extract
1 teaspoon ground cinnamon

Fruit Topping
1 bag fresh cranberries
1/2 cup dried cranberries
1 cup sugar
1 teaspoon orange zest, chopped

Preheat the oven to 375 degrees F. Grind or process the graham crackers until fine, and place in a bowl with the sugar, cinnamon, and pecans. Add just enough butter until the mixture begins to clump together. Press the crumbs on the bottom of a 9 inch spring form pan. Bake the crust until it begins to brown and set, about 8 minutes. Let cool. Once cool, wrap the spring form pan with aluminum foil, and place in a larger baking pan. Pour enough water into the larger pan until the water comes half way up the sides of the spring form pan. Reduce the oven temperature to 325 degrees. F.

Beat the cream cheese with the sugar until light and fluffy. Add the rum, nutmeg, and vanilla and mix well. Add the eggs, one at a time, beating at slow speed just until blended. Over beating at this stage may cause cracking as the cheesecake cools. Pour the filling into the crust, and bake for 1 hour and 15 minutes, or until the cheesecake is set around the outer edges with only 3 inches or so of the center still a little soft and wobbly. Turn off the oven, and leave the oven door open. Cool the cheesecake slowly in this manner for 45 minutes. Remove from the oven.

Turn the oven to 400 degrees F. Mix together the baked topping ingredients, and pour these over the cheesecake. Smooth lightly with a spoon. Bake for about 10 minutes or until the topping begins to set. Remove, and cool at room temperature for 45 minutes. Refrigerate for 4 hours.

To make the fruit topping, combine the fresh and dried cranberries, sugar, and orange zest in a saucepan. Bring to a boil, and reduce the heat to medium. Continue cooking for about 25 minutes, or until the cranberries have softened and the sauce has thickened. Place the sauce in a blender or food processor, and blend until smooth. Strain the sauce through a sieve so you have a clear topping. Cool to room temperature and then pour over the cheesecake. Continue to refrigerate for another 4 hours or overnight. Remove the spring form pan sides carefully, and cut the cheesecake into small slices to serve.

Italian Apple Cake

Don't get caught off guard by the title of this recipe. This dessert is very different than most American cakes. The abundant amount of apples are coated with a minimal amount of batter which is made of yeast and whipped egg whites.

A touch of cinnamon and a powdered sugar glaze enhances the results of this unusual but delicious Italian "cake."

2 large egg yolks
1/3 cup all-purpose flour
1 tablespoon sugar
Pinch of salt
1/6 oz dried yeast
1/4 cup milk
2 lb apples, peeled and thinly sliced
2 large egg whites

Butter a 10-inch diameter cake pan. Preheat the oven to 325 degrees F. Beat the egg yolks in a large bowl. Mix in the flour, sugar, salt, yeast and milk. Add the apples and stir to coat. Using an electric mixer with clean dry beaters, whip the egg whites in another large bowl until stiff peaks form. Gently fold the beaten egg whites into the apple mixture.

Immediately transfer the mixture to the prepared cake pan and bake until a skewer inserted into the center of the cake comes out dry, about 45 minutes.

Allow to cool before serving.

Italian Cheesecake

Crust
1 1/2 cups graham crackers or shortbread crumbs
1 tablespoon brown sugar
1 tablespoon ground cinnamon
1/4 cup unsalted butter, melted and cooled

Filling
1 lb cream cheese
1 cup ricotta cheese
4 eggs
1/3 cup unsweetened cocoa powder
1 teaspoon vanilla extract
1 cup sugar
3 tablespoons brewed strong black coffee
2 teaspoons ground cinnamon

Topping
1 cup sour cream
1/2 cup superfine sugar
1 tablespoon cocoa powder
1 teaspoon cinnamon

Line a 9-inch springform cake pan with foil and lightly grease the sides.

FOR THE CRUST: Combine the cracker or shortbread crumbs, brown sugar, and cinnamon in a bowl, then stir in the melted butter. Press the mixture into the base of the prepared pan.

Preheat the oven to 325 degrees F.

FOR THE FILLING: Place the cream cheese, ricotta cheese, eggs, cocoa powder, and vanilla in a food processor and process until smooth. Add the sugar, coffee, and cinnamon and continue to beat for 10 minutes or until the mixture is combined.

Pour into the crust-lined pan and bake for 1 hour, or until just firm to touch. Allow the cake to stand for 5 minutes before spreading on the topping.   *23*

FOR THE TOPPING: Combine the sour cream, sugar, cocoa powder, and cinnamon in a bowl and stir thoroughly. Spread over the cooked cheesecake and return to the oven for 10-15 minutes, or until just set. Allow the cheesecake to cool completely in the pan before refrigerating overnight.

TO SERVE: Run a knife around the edge of the pan and gently remove the sides.

Italian Fruit Cake

Delicate coils of pastry surround raisins and walnuts in this traditional Calabrian treat.

For Filling

2 pounds of raisins
2 pounds coarsely chopped walnuts
1 cup whiskey
1 1/2 cups sugar
3 tablespoons cinnamon
juice of 1 orange
dash of Anisette

Combine all filling ingredients in a glass bowl, cover and let sit overnight, stirring occasionally.

Dough

7 cups all-purpose flour
1 1/2 cup white wine
5 eggs
zest from 1 lemon and 1 orange
2 cups sugar
1 cup oil
1/2 cup whiskey
2 teaspoons vanilla extract
dash of cinnamon
1 tablespoon baking soda
Toothpicks

Topping

1 cup honey
colored sprinkles

Make a mound of the flour on a pastry board or counter. Make a well in the center, and using a fork, begin to add in the remaining ingredients until you have created a dough. **25**

Knead with additional flour as needed until smooth. Divide into 6 Equal sized balls. Covering the rest of the balls, take one and begin to run it through a pasta machine to flatten. Continue to lightly flour and pass through increasingly narrow openings, until the dough is between 1/8 to 1/4 inch thick. Place on the counter, and using a scalloped pastry wheel, run it along the outside edges of each side of the dough.

Next using the pastry wheel, cut the strip of dough in half lengthwise into two ribbons. On each half of the ribbon, sprinkle on some of the walnut, raisin mixture and fold to close. Starting at one end, begin to roll up the dough into a coil, using toothpicks to support it as needed.

Continue until you have an 8 inch cake, using some of the second strip as needed. Continue using all of the dough up in this manner.

Preheat the oven to 325 degrees F. Place the cakes on a lightly floured baking sheet and bake for about 35 minutes or until lightly browned. Melt the honey in a pot and brush each of the cakes lightly over the top. Sprinkle with the candy sprinkles and bake an additional 10 minutes. Let cool completely and then wrap in foil to store. To serve, remove the toothpicks and cut into wedges.

Italian Rice Cake

3 cups milk
3/4 cup Arborio rice
4 eggs, beaten
1/2 cup sugar
1/4 cup chopped pistachios
1/4 cup chopped walnuts
1/4 cup pine nuts
1/4 cup candied orange peel, finely diced
1/4 teaspoon vanilla
2 tablespoon butter, room temperature
zest of 1/2 lemon
confectioners sugar to dusting

In a saucepan over medium heat, bring milk just to a boil.
Add rice, reduce to low, cover and simmer about 30 minutes.

Remove from heat and allow to cool.

Stir the eggs into the cooled rice mixture. Add the remaining
ingredients, except the confectioners sugar.

Preheat oven to 350 degrees F. Butter a 10-inch round cake pan.
Pour the rice mixture into the prepared pan. Bake 1 hour until a
skewer inserted in the center comes out clean.

Cool to lukewarm and unmold onto a serving dish.
Before serving, dust with confectioners sugar.

Italian Rice Pie I

9 eggs
1 1/2 cups white sugar
2 pounds ricotta cheese
1 teaspoon vanilla extract
2 cups heavy whipping cream
1 cup cooked white rice
1 (15 ounce) can crushed pineapple, drained

Beat eggs in very large bowl. Add sugar, mixing well. Stir in cheese and vanilla until smooth and creamy. Add heavy cream and stir. Fold in cooked rice and crushed pineapple.

Pour into a 9 x 13 inch buttered pan.

Bake at 325 degrees F (165 degrees C) for one hour. Check by inserting clean knife into center. If the pie is done, knife will come out clean. Top should be golden brown.

Refrigerate until thoroughly cooled.

Italian Rice Pie II

Sweet rice pie is a dessert traditionally served on Easter by many Italian families.

2 1/2 cups all-purpose flour

1 tablespoon baking powder

1/4 cup butter

1/4 cup white sugar

3 eggs

1/2 teaspoon vanilla extract

1/2 cup uncooked white rice

1 cup water

1 quart milk

1 (15 ounce) container ricotta cheese

1 1/2 cups white sugar

1 tablespoon lemon juice

1 tablespoon grated lemon zest

6 eggs

In a medium bowl, mix together flour and baking powder; set aside. In a large bowl, cream butter and 1/2 cup sugar until light and fluffy. Beat in eggs, one at a time, then stir in vanilla.

Beat in flour mixture. Divide dough in half and shape into balls. Roll out to fit 2 (10 inch) pie plates.

In a saucepan, bring water to a boil. Add rice and stir. Reduce heat, cover and simmer for 20 minutes. Stir in milk. Continue cooking, stirring frequently, until thickened. Set aside to cool. Preheat oven to 325 degrees F (165 degrees C).

In a large bowl, beat together ricotta cheese, 1 1/2 cups sugar, lemon juice, lemon zest and eggs. Blend in cooled rice mixture. Pour into pie shells.

Bake in preheated oven for 90 minutes, or until filling is set and top is golden brown.

Italian Rum Cake

3 egg yolks
1 cup sugar
2 1/4 cups all-purpose flour
2 cups milk
1/2 lemon; grated peel only
1 cup butter; room temperature
4 eggs
3/4 cup sour cream
1 tsp vanilla extract
1/2 teaspoon. nutmeg
1/4 teaspoon baking soda
1/4 teaspoon salt
1/2 cup dark rum

Preheat oven to 350° F.

Beat the yolks and 1/4 cup sugar together in a mixing bowl and slowly add 1/4 cup flour.

Meanwhile, place the milk in a small pot and bring to the brink of boiling. Slowly pour the milk over the yolk mixture, then pour the whole thing back into the pot. Place over medium heat and cook, stirring constantly, until the mixture thickens. Remove from the heat and mix in the lemon peel. Scrape into a plastic container, cover and place in the refrigerator to chill.

Running your mixer at high speed, cream butter and remaining sugar together in a mixer fitted with a paddle. Add the eggs 1 at a time, waiting until the previous 1 has been absorbed.

Add the sour cream and mix until incorporated. Add vanilla, nutmeg, baking soda and salt. Decrease the speed to medium, add remaining flour and mix an additional minute.

Scrape the batter into a 1-quart round or rectangular cake pan, leaving 1/2-inch space at the top. Place on the middle rack of the oven for 50-to-60 minutes.

The cake is done when the surface cracks and a toothpick inserted into the center comes out clean. Remove cake from the oven and let cool for 15 minutes before unmolding onto rack. When the cake is completely cool, slice it into 6 layers.

Place the first layer on a cake platter and sprinkle with some of the rum. Cover the layer with some of the custard mixture. Place the second layer on top of the custard, sprinkle with rum and cover with more custard.

Continue until the cake is assembled. Lightly spread the custard all over the surface of the cake. Refrigerate for 2 hours before serving.

Jam Tart

For the Pastry Dough

1/4 cup sugar
8 tablespoons (1 stick) unsalted butter, diced
2 large eggs
1 teaspoon vanilla extract
1 teaspoon grated lemon zest
Pinch of salt
2 cups all-purpose flour

For the Filling

1 cup strawberry, raspberry, or blueberry jam

For the Egg Wash:
1 large egg
1 teaspoon water
Pinch of salt

TO MAKE THE DOUGH IN AN ELECTRIC MIXER: In the bowl of a standing mixer or with a hand-held blender, cream the sugar and butter together. Mix in the eggs, vanilla, and lemon zest until smooth. Add the salt and flour, and mix until the dough comes together. Be careful not to overmix the dough or it will be tough

TO MAKE THE DOUGH BY HAND: Place the flour, salt, and sugar in a bowl. With your fingertips, work the butter into the dry ingredients until it resembles coarse meal. In a small bowl, lightly whisk together the eggs, vanilla, and lemon zest. Add the wet ingredients to the flour-butter combination and mix until the dough comes together. Form the dough into a disk, wrap it in plastic, and chill for at least 1 hour or overnight.

TO ROLL THE DOUGH: Cut off a third of the dough and set it aside for the lattice top of the tart. Press the remaining dough into a disk, and roll it out on a lightly floured surface into a 12-inch round about 1/4-inch thick. Trim any rough edges, transfer the

round to a parchment-lined cookie sheet, and chill while you roll out the other piece of dough into a 10-x 6-inch rectangle. To make the strips for the lattice top, cut 12 even 10-inch strips. Cut 2 strips in half to make 5-inch lengths. You will have a total of 14 pieces.

Remove the pastry round from the refrigerator and, with a spatula, spread the jam over the surface of the dough, leaving an inch border all around. Place 7 strips of pastry over the jam. Use 2 of the short strips at the ends. Trim off any excess dough that drapes over the edge of the tart. Turn the tart and repeat the procedure with the remaining strips of dough to form a lattice pattern. Fold the border of the tart over to cover the ends of the lattice, making a 1-inch rim.

TO MAKE THE EGG WASH: In a small bowl, whisk together the ingredients. With a pastry brush, lightly brush the dough with the egg wash. Press the tines of a fork into the edge of the crust to make a decorative pattern. Chill the tart for 1 hour before baking.

Preheat the oven to 350 degrees F. Bake the tart for 30 to 35 minutes in the upper third of the oven, until the crust is lightly browned. Remove the tart from the oven and slide it onto a rack to cool. Chill for 1 hour and serve.

No-Bake Cranberry Cheesecake

This is a nice, light textured cheesecake that would make a perfect ending to a holiday meal with its pretty cranberry, jewel colored topping.

For Crust

2 cup graham cracker crumbs
3 tablespoons sugar
7 tablespoons unsalted butter, melted

Cake Filling

1 pound cream cheese, softened
6 tablespoons white sugar
2 teaspoons vanilla extract
2 cups chilled heavy cream (whipping cream)
1 package (2 teaspoons) unflavored gelatin

Topping

1 cup Ruby Port
1 cup sugar
2 cups fresh cranberries
1/2 teaspoon cinnamon

Preheat oven to 350 degrees F. To make the crust, mix together the topping ingredients, and press into the bottom and up the sides about 2 inches of a 10 inch springform pan. Bake until the crust is set, about 10 to 12 minutes. Remove from the oven, and let cool to room temperature.

To make the filling, sprinkle the gelatin over 1/2 cup of the heavy cream in a bowl to soften for 5 minutes. Heat the remaining cream in a saucepan, and once simmering, remove from the heat. Add the gelatin mixture and stir to mix well. Allow the mixture to cool to room temperature, about 45 minutes.

In a large bowl, beat the softened cream cheese and sugar until light and fluffy. Add the vanilla extract and mix well. Add the cream and gelatin mixture to the cream cheese in the bowl, and mix just until combined. Pour this into the prepared crust, and refrigerate for at least 6 hours, or up to one day ahead of serving.

To make the cranberry topping, heat the sugar and port together in a saucepan until boiling. Reduce the heat to a simmer, and add the cranberries and cinnamon. Stir to mix, and cook until the cranberries begin to pop, about 10 minutes. Remove from the heat, and refrigerate until cold and thick.

To serve, cut into thin slices, and spoon a good sized helping of the cranberry mixture over each slice of cheesecake.

Olive Oil Cake

When baked, olive oil has a rich and somewhat mysterious flavor.
This cake is high and handsome, much like a chiffon cake. In fact,
call this chiffon cake--people often balk at the idea, but not the
taste, of an olive oil cake. Serve this delicate confection with
dessert wine or sherry and accompany with sliced nectarines,
pears, berries, and whipped cream flavored with apricot preserves.

4 eggs, separated, plus 1 egg white, at room temperature
1 cup sugar
1 teaspoon vanilla
1 tablespoon orange flower water
Finely grated zest of 1 orange and 1 lemon
1/2 teaspoon salt
1/2 cup plus 2 tablespoons olive oil
1 1/3 cups milk
2 1/2 cups sifted cake flour
2 teaspoons baking powder
Powdered sugar

Preheat oven to 375 degrees F. Oil or butter and flour a 10-inch
springform or bundt pan.

Beat the egg whites until they form soft peaks, then gradually add
1/3 cup of the sugar and continue beating until firm peaks are
formed. Scrape them into a large bowl and set aside. In the same
mixing bowl, don't bother to rinse it, beat the yolks with the
remaining sugar until thick and light colored. Lower the speed,
add the flavorings and salt, then gradually pour in the olive oil.
The batter will be thick, like mayonnaise. Slowly add the milk,
then whisk in the flour and baking powder. Reach thoroughly
around the bottom of the bowl to make sure everything is well
mixed. Fold in the egg whites. Scrape the batter into the prepared
pan.

Bake in the center of the oven for 25 minutes. Reduce the temperature to 325 degrees F and bake for 40 minutes more until a cake tester comes out clean and the cake has begun to pull away from the sides. (It's better to err on the side of overbaking than underbaking this cake.) Let cool in the pan for 10 minutes. Remove the rim of invert, if using a bundt pan, onto a cooling rack. When cool, gently transfer the cake to plate and dust with powdered sugar.

Panettone

A very tasty holiday addition to any family sweet's table. Usually one would use a round, tall sided panettone pan which can be found at kitchen specialty stores, but almost any casserole or bread pan could be used.

10-11 cups all-purpose flour
2 cups sugar
8 eggs
2 cups milk
1/2 cup warm water
3 pkgs. active dry yeast
peel of 1 lemon, finely grated
1 cup candied fruit
3/4 cup raisins
1/3 cup oil
1/2 cup shortening
2 teaspoon vanilla extract
1/2 cup Anisette liquor

First dissolve the yeast in the water and let sit until bubbly. Mix together the rest of the ingredients, adding enough flour to make workable dough. Knead until you have smooth, elastic dough, about 8 minutes. Cover and let rise for 10 - 12 hours. Place on a floured board, and cut into four equal pieces. Place each piece in a buttered pan. Let rise another 8 hours or until fully risen. Bake at 300 degrees F. until golden brown, about 1 hour.

Panettone Farcito

In this tasty holiday recipe, traditional panettone is stuffed with a creamy filling.

This is a traditional Christmas bread recipe from Milano which can now not only be found across Italy, but worldwide. There are many variations to recipes using a prepared panettone and this is one of my favorites. You can also cut out the center and fill with a prepared mousse or ice cream and freeze until ready to serve.

1 (2 pound) Panettone (store bought is fine)
4 oz. toasted sliced almonds
4 oz. Cointreau or other orange liqueur
1 cup heavy cream
1/2 granulated sugar
2 tablespoons gelatin
2 teaspoons vanilla extract
2 cups milk
6 egg yolks
2 teaspoons corn starch

To Garnish (optional)

3/4 cup sugar
powdered sugar

Slice the panettone into 5 1 inch equal rounds, discarding one layer from the center. Soften the gelatin in a little milk. Heat the milk in a pan over medium heat. Whisk together the egg yolks, sugar and cornstarch in a small bowl. Add a little of the hot milk to the egg mixture and mix well. Add this mixture to the rest of the milk in the pan, and whisk until smooth over low heat. Add the softened gelatin, vanilla and mix. Refrigerate until cool. Whip the heavy cream and fold into the gelatin mixture once it is cool. Chill for one hour.

Dilute the cointreau with a few teaspoons of water, and lightly brush the top of the panettone rounds, reserving some of this mixture for the outside. Start to reassemble the panettone, by spreading the bottom layer with some of the cream mixture. Continue to reassemble using each layer and all the cream mixture. Brush the exterior sides with the cointreau and lightly press on the almond slices. Refrigerate until ready to serve.

Optional Garnish: For a very impressive presentation, melt the 3/4 cup of sugar until boiling with just a little water. Continue stirring until it has completely caramelized. Take one strand at a time, and stretch it over two wooden spoon handles until you have a pile of sugar strands. Arrange this on top of the panettone, and sprinkle with a light coating of powdered sugar.

Other suggestions for serving are to serve each slice with a drizzle of chocolate sauce, or a spoonful of mixed berries sweetened with a little sugar.

Pear Pecan Coffee Cake

Moist and slightly sweet, this cinnamon flavored coffee cake would be great any time of the day.

This is a really moist, tasty cake that isn't too sweet. It would be nice after dinner as a dessert warmed with a scoop of vanilla ice cream, for breakfast as a traditional coffee cake or as a midmorning pick-me-up. I created this cake one day trying to use up some pears in my fridge that were ripening too quickly, as well as some sour cream I wanted to finish up. I added some cinnamon, pecans and a hint of lemon and ended up with this nice cake.

Fruit Filling

4 ripe pears
1 cup chopped pecans
3 tablespoons sugar
1 tablespoon cinnamon

Coffee Cake

2 large eggs
2 cups sour cream (or creme fraiche or yoghurt)
1 tablespoon vanilla extract
8 ounces unsalted butter at room temperature
1 tablespoon finely chopped lemon peel
1 tablespoon baking powder
dash of salt
2 cups granulated sugar
3 cups all-purpose flour

Prepare your pan by buttering either a 10" cake pan, or a 10" bundt pan.

To prepare the filling, peel and core the pears. Cut the fruit into 1/2 inch dice. Mix together with the rest of the topping ingredients, and set aside.

Preheat oven to 350 degrees F. Mix together the eggs and sour cream with the vanilla extract. In a large mixing bowl, beat the butter and lemon zest until light and fluffy. Add the sugar and continue beating another 3 to 4 minutes. Add the egg mixture, and on low speed mix well with the butter mixture.

Add the flour, baking powder and salt, and mix just until it is combined. Pour half the mixture into your prepared pan, and spread the filling mixture over top. Pour the rest of the batter over the filling and carefully spread evenly. Bake for about 1 hour, or until a cake tester comes out clean. Serve either warm, or at room temperature.

Pignoli (Pine) Nut Pie

Pignoli nuts are an Italian version of the pine nut.

1/2 cup white sugar
3/4 cup packed brown sugar
2 eggs, beaten
1 1/2 teaspoons vanilla extract
1 tablespoon all-purpose flour
1 tablespoon heavy whipping cream
8 tablespoons unsalted butter, melted
3/4 cup pignoli nuts
1 (9 inch) pie shell

Combine the white sugar, brown sugar, eggs, vanilla, flour, cream, and melted butter in a bowl. Whisk until well blended. Fold in the pignoli nuts. Pour filling into the pie crust.

Bake at 350 degrees F (175 degrees C) for 50 minutes.

Pine Nut Cake

One of the most traditional of all ingredients in Italian cooking is the pine nut. Pine nuts are mainly gathered in Tuscany, along the sea shore where there are whole forests of pines. One of the most beautiful is the Migliarino forest near Pisa.

Pine nuts are used in sweet dishes, often with raisins or candied fruits, in savory dishes, and even with fish and meat. Normally they are used raw, but occasionally as in this recipe, they are first toasted in the oven.

4 eggs, separated
3/4 cup superfine sugar
1/3 cup butter
2 1/2 cups all-purpose flour
6 oz pine nuts
1 tablespoon powdered sugar

In a bowl, beat the egg yolks with half the sugar. In another bowl, beat the remaining sugar with the butter. Gently stir the two mixtures together. Gradually add this to the flour, mixing in a little at a time to avoid lumps forming. Beat the eggwhites until stiff and gently fold them into the mixture, taking care to retain as much air as possible. Scatter the pine nuts over a baking sheet. Toast in a preheated 350 degrees F oven until they begin to color. Grind 5 oz of them in a blender and reserve the remainder. Fold the ground nuts into the batter. Butter and flour a 9 inch springform pan and fill it with the batter. Bake at 350 degrees F for about 45 minutes, or until a skewer inserted in the center comes out dry.

Turn the cake out onto a serving plate. Decorate the top with the remaining pine nuts, sprinkle with the powdered sugar and serve.

Plum Cake

Most trattorias take advantage of the abundance of seasonal fruits by offering them in desserts. In place of the plump summer plums that crown this delectable cake, you can use apricots, nectarines or blueberries. Whatever your selection, make sure the fruit is ripe but firm, as it will soften during baking.

6 tablespoons unsalted butter, at room temperature
1/3 cup plus 1 teaspoon granulated sugar
2 extra-large eggs, separated, at room temperature
1 cup unbleached all-purpose flour
2 1/2 teaspoons baking powder
1/4 cup heavy cream
1/4 cup water
2 teaspoons almond extract
1 1/2 teaspoons vanilla extract
2 ripe plums, peeled, pitted and sliced into sixths
Confectioners' sugar

Preheat an oven to 400 degrees F. Butter and flour a 9-inch cake pan or a tart pan with a removable bottom.

In a bowl, using an electric mixer set on medium speed, beat together the butter and the 1/3 cup granulated sugar until smooth and fluffy, 2-3 minutes. Add the egg yolks and beat until very smooth.

In a small bowl, stir together the flour and baking powder. In another small bowl, stir together the cream, water and almond and vanilla extracts. Stir the flour mixture into the butter mixture alternately with the cream mixture, beginning and ending with the flour mixture. Do not overmix.

In a clean bowl, using clean beaters, whip the egg whites until they form very soft peaks. Sprinkle in the 1 teaspoon granulated sugar and continue to beat until semisoft peaks form. Using a rubber spatula or whisk, fold the beaten egg whites into the batter, breaking apart any lumps. Pour the batter into the prepared pan and level the surface. **45**

Arrange the plums in a circle on the top of the batter. Place in the center of the oven and immediately reduce the heat to 350 degrees F. Bake until the cake pulls away from the sides of the pan and a toothpick inserted into the center comes out clean, 35-40 minutes. Transfer to a rack and let cool slightly.

If using a cake pan, run a knife blade around the edge of the pan to loosen the cake sides, invert onto the rack and then turn the cake right side up. If using a tart pan, remove the pan sides.

Place the cake on a serving plate and using a fine-mesh sieve, sift confectioners' sugar evenly over the top. Serve warm or at room temperature.

Ricotta Cheesecake

Crust

1-1/2 cups amaretti cookie crumbs
5 tablespoons unsalted butter, melted
For Filling:
1/4 cup Amaretto
1/2 cup chopped dried apricots
3 cups whole-milk ricotta cheese
1/4 cup all-purpose flour
2/3 cup sugar
1/8 teaspoon ground mace
1 teaspoon vanilla extract
4 large eggs, separated
salt

TO MAKE CRUST: Combine the cookie crumbs with 4
tablespoons of the butter. Brush a 10-inch springform pan with the
remaining butter and then press in the crust. Refrigerate while you
prepare the filling.

Preheat the oven to 350 degrees F.

TO MAKE FILLING: In a small pan, heat the Amaretto with the
apricots to plump the fruit. Set aside. In a food processor, pulse
the ricotta until it is creamy. Remove from the processor and mix
it in a bowl together with the flour, sugar, mace, vanilla, egg yolks,
and soaked apricots.

In a stainless-steel bowl, whisk the egg whites with a pinch of salt
to soft peaks. With a rubber spatula, fold a third of the beaten egg
whites into the ricotta filling to lighten the batter. Fold in the
remaining egg whites.

Pour the filling into the chilled crust and bake for 1 hour, or until
the filling is golden brown and set. Remove from the oven and
cool on a rack.

Ricotta Cheesecake with Mixed Berry Topping

This ricotta cake is very moist, and is set off wonderfully with a mixture of ripe, sweet berries.

Cake

2 pounds ricotta cheese
2/3 cup white sugar
1/3 cup all-purpose flour
6 eggs
2 teaspoons vanilla extract
1/8 teaspoon salt

Sauce

1 cup raspberries
1 cup blueberries
1 cup strawberries
2 tablespoons sugar
1 tablespoon balsamic vinegar

Wash the berries, and pick through, discarding any that have spoiled. Remove the tops off of the stawberries, and slice them into a bowl. Add the bleberries and raspberries, as well as the sugar and vinegar. Cover and set aside.

Preheat oven to 300 degrees F (150 degrees C). Set rack in the middle of the oven. Butter and flour a 9 1/2 inch springform pan, and tap out excess flour. Place the ricotta in a large mixing bowl, and beat it until smooth. Beat the sugar and flour together thoroughly into the ricotta. Beat in the eggs at low speed, 1 at a time. Blend in the vanilla, and salt. Pour batter into the prepared pan. Bake in the center of the oven for about 1 1/4 to 1 1/2 hours, until a light golden color. Make sure the center is fairly firm, and the point of a sharp knife inserted in the center comes out clean. Cool on a wire rack. It will sink slightly as it cools. Cover, and chill till serving time. To serve, cut into thin slices, and spoon a good sized helping of the berry mixture over each slice of cheesecake.

48

Ricotta Jam Tart

A sweet, rich ricotta tart with a layer of jam running through the center. Generally after a complete meal, Italians prefer fresh fruit. When they do partake of a dessert however, it is often a small sliver of a nutty or rich tart such as this ricotta tart with a layer of blueberry jam. Use any variety or flavor of jam you prefer.

Pastry (use your favorite pastry crust, or the one here)
1 3/4 cups all-Purpose flour
1/4 cups sugar
1/2 teaspoon baking powder
1/2 cup chilled, sweet butter
1 whole egg and one additional egg yolk

Filling
2 cups whole milk ricotta cheese
3 eggs
1/3 cup sugar
1 teaspoon vanilla extract
1 cup fruit jam (I prefer blueberry)
1 (10-11 inch) tart pan with removable bottom
powdered sugar

Prepare the crust first, by first mixing the sugar, flour and baking powder. Cut the butter into this mixture until it resembles small peas. Whisk together your egg and egg yolk, and add this to the dry ingredients. Combine just until the dough comes together. Do not over mix. If the mixture seems a bit dry, add a tablespoon or so of ice water. Wrap this dough in plastic wrap and refrigerate for at least 30 minutes, no longer than 2 hours.
Preheat the oven to 375 degrees F. Roll the dough on a lightly floured surface into a 10-11 inch round, depending the size of your chosen pan. Transfer the dough carefully to the pan and trim.
To prepare the filling, mix together the ricotta, sugar, eggs and vanilla until well blended. Spread the jam across the bottom of your pie pan, and pour the ricotta mixture overtop.
Bake for about 55 minutes or until golden. Remove from the heat and cool. When cool, remove from the pan rim, sprinkle with powdered sugar and serve.

49

Ricotta Lemon Cake with Blueberry Topping

Moist, light, and lemon flavored, this cake is perfect for a topping of sweetened berries. A small slice of heaven to end your meal.

Cake

2 cups sugar
1 cup softened butter
1/2 cup ricotta cheese
1/2 cup milk
3 cups all-purpose flour
1 1/2 teaspoons lemon extract
zest of 1 lemon, finely chopped
4 large eggs
powdered sugar for topping

Topping

3 cups blueberries
3/4 cup sugar
1 teaspoon lemon juice

For the cake, preheat the oven to 350 degrees F. Butter and flour a 9" cake pan. In a bowl, mix together the butter and sugar until fluffy. Add the eggs, lemon extract, milk, ricotta, flour and lemon zest, and beat well for 2 minutes on high speed. Pour into your prepared pan, and bake 45-50 minutes, or until a toothpick inserted in the center comes out clean. Cool.

To prepare the topping, combine the blueberries, lemon, sugar and 1/2 cup of water, and cook until thickened. Remove and cool. Once the cake has cooled, dust lightly with the powdered sugar. Serve a small slice with a spoonful of blueberry topping.

Ricotta Pancakes

At one time these pancakes used to be filled with a creamy cheese much fatter than ricotta called mascarpone. Small pieces of chocolate are often used instead of the raisins, perhaps mixed with candied fruit or candied orange peel. Ricotta pancakes are a northern version of the Sicilian cannoli.

2 oz golden raisins
3 eggs
3 tablespoons all-purpose flour
Salt
1/3 cup milk
8 oz ricotta cheese
1 tablespoon superfine sugar
3 tablespoons cream
1 1/2 tablespoons butter

In a bowl, soak the raisins. Beat the eggs in a bowl. Add the flour and whisk until smooth. Add the salt. Slowly add the milk and whisk well. Set aside to rest for a few minutes. Drain the raisins and pat dry.

Push the ricotta through a sieve into a bowl. Stir in the sugar, raisins and the cream.

Melt the butter in a small nonstick skillet. Pour in a small amount of the batter and tilt the pan until the bottom is evenly coated with the batter. Cook the pancake on one side; turn carefully and cook on the other side. Continue making the pancakes in this manner until all of the batter is used.

Fill the pancakes with the ricotta cream, rolling them around it. Arrange on a serving dish and serve.

Roman Cheesecake

Italian ricotta cheese is less runny than what we have in America. In order to duplicate the Italian texture we blended farmer's cheese with ricotta cheese. To help set the cake, we also added a couple of tablespoonfuls of flour and an egg. I like the tang of the dried cherries, but the cake works as well with golden raisins.

For the Dough:

2 1/2 cups all-purpose flour
3/4 cup sugar
1/4 teaspoon salt
1/4 pound unsalted butter, at room temperature
2 large eggs, lightly beaten
1 tablespoon or more ice water

For the Filling:

1 carton (15 ounces) whole milk ricotta cheese
1 package (7.5 ounces) farmers cheese
1/2 cup sugar
2 tablespoons flour
1 egg, lightly beaten
1/4 cup Romana Sambuca Liqueur
1/2 cup pine nuts, preferably toasted (see Note)
1/4 cup finely diced candied orange peel or other dried fruit
1 cup dried cherries, cranberries or golden raisins
Egg wash: 1 egg yolk beaten with 1 tablespoon of milk
2 tablespoons Confectioners' sugar for garnish

You'll need a round cake pan, preferably with a loose bottom, 9 inches in diameter and 1 1/2 inches deep.

TO MAKE THE DOUGH: In the bowl of a food processor, combine the flour, sugar, salt and process until blended. Add the butter and process until broken into the flour. Add the eggs and ice water to the flour and process, by pulsing several times, until the dough comes together. If the dough seems dry, add another teaspoon or so of ice water. Turn the dough onto a board and gather it into a ball. Flatten the dough slightly, wrap it in waxed paper and refrigerate for 30 minutes.

Preheat the oven to 375 degrees F.

Flour a pastry board and rolling pin. Remove 2/3's of the dough and roll it into a circle about 1/4-inch thick and 11 inches in diameter. Line the cake pan with the dough, pressing it into the bottom and up the sides of the pan. If it breaks apart, don't worry; just press it back into shape. Roll the remaining 1/3 of dough into a circle about 3/8 -inch thick and 10 inches in diameter. Divide this circle into 10 strips, each about 1/2-inch wide; this will be for the lattice top.

TO MAKE FILLING: In a food processor, combine the ricotta and farmer's cheese, sugar, flour, egg and Sambuca and process until smooth. Transfer the filling to a mixing bowl and fold in the pine nuts, candied orange peel and cherries, or golden raisins and transfer this to the dough-lined cake pan.

Lay 5 strips of dough across the ricotta filling and set the other 5 strips across them, at a 45 degree angle, to form a lattice. With a pastry brush, paint the lattice top and edges with the egg wash.

Set the cake pan on a baking pan and bake for 1 hour or until the filling has set and the crust is golden. Remove the cake and cool it thoroughly on a rack before unmolding. Right before serving, shake the confectioners' sugar through a sieve to completely coat the top.

To toast the pine nuts, set them in a 400 degrees F. oven for about 10 minutes. Keep an eye on them; they turn from golden to burned in seconds.

Sicilian Dessert Cake

Cake

1/2 cup butter
1/2 cup sugar
2 eggs
1 teaspoon vanilla extract
1 1/4 cups self-rising flour
1/4 cup all-purpose flour
1/4 teaspoon salt
1/2 cup milk

Filling

1 cup ricotta cheese
3/4 cup cream
1/4 cup sugar
2 tablespoons chopped glaceed cherries
1 tablespoon chopped candied citrus peel
1 tablespoon chopped glaceed pineapple
1 tablespoon chopped glaceed apricots
Grated zest (rind) of 1/2 orange
2 oz semisweet chocolate, chopped
2 tablespoons Cointreau or other orange liqueur

Icing

4 oz semisweet dark chocolate
2 tablespoons brewed strong black coffee
1/3 cup unsalted butter, cut into small pieces

Preheat the oven to 350 degrees F. Butter a 9 x 5-inch loaf pan and line with parchment or waxed (greaseproof) paper.

FOR THE CAKE: Cream the butter and sugar until light and fluffy. Whisk the eggs with the vanilla. Combine with the butter mixture, stirring well. Sift together the flours and salt and fold into the butter mixture alternately with the milk.

Pour the batter into the prepared pan and bake for 40 minutes, or until a skewer inserted in the middle of the cake comes out clean. Turn out onto a wire rack and cool completely, preferably overnight.

If the top of the cake is not flat, trim away any domed part until the top is flat. Cut the cake horizontally into 4 layers.

FOR THE FILLING: Place the ricotta cheese in the bowl of a food processor and process until smooth. Add the cream and sugar and process until well combined. Transfer to a bowl and fold in all the other ingredients, except the Cointreau.

Line the cake pan with an overhanging piece of parchment or waxed paper. Place the bottom layer of cake back in the pan and brush with a little of the Cointreau. Cover with one-third of the ricotta filling. Top with the next layer or cake and repeat until the remaining Cointreau, ricotta filling, and 2 layers of cake have been used, ending with a layer of cake. Refrigerate for at least 1 hour.

FOR THE ICING: Place the chocolate in a double boiler with the coffee. Stir until melted. Add the butter and stir until smooth. Remove from the heat and refrigerate for 15 minutes, or until the chocolate cools to a spreading consistency. Gently remove the cake from the pan and spread with the chocolate icing.

Serve immediately or refrigerate overnight until ready to serve.

Strawberry Cheesecake

Jewish and Italian immigrants alike brought their own distinctive versions of cheesecake to America. The kind most likely to be found in diners is more typically Jewish, and is now widely known as New York style. If you like, make this particular recipe with a combination of jams and fruit; apricots or plums are especially good.

For Crust
1 1/2 cups graham crackers crumbs
2 tablespoons granulated sugar
6 tablespoons unsalted butter, melted

For Filling
Three 8-ounce packages cream cheese, room temperature
1 1/4 cups granulated sugar
6 large eggs, at room temperature
2 cups sour cream, at room temperature
1/3 cup all-purpose flour, sifted
2 teaspoons vanilla extract
Finely grated zest and juice of 1 lemon
1/2 cup strawberry jam
1/2 cup finely chopped, strawberries
12 whole strawberries, hulled

FOR CRUST: Preheat an oven to 350 degrees F. Grease a springform pan 9 1/2 inches in diameter and 3 inches deep with butter. In a bowl, combine the crumbs, sugar and melted butter, breaking up any large crumbs and mixing well. Firmly press the mixture evenly over the bottom and about 2 inches up the sides of the prepared pan.

FOR FILLING: In a large bowl, break the cream cheese into pieces. Using an electric mixer set on medium speed, beat until soft and creamy, about 3 minutes. Add the sugar and beat until the mixture is smooth, 1-2 minutes. Add the eggs, one at a time, beating well after each addition. Reduce the speed to low and beat in the sour cream, flour, vanilla and lemon zest and juice until thoroughly blended.

56

Remove 1 cup of the batter and place it in a small mixing bowl. Add the strawberry jam, mixing thoroughly, and then gently mix in the chopped strawberries. Pour this mixture into the rest of the batter and stir just until incorporated. Pour into the prepared pan and jiggle the pan until the batter is level.

Bake for 1 hour. Turn off the heat and allow the cheesecake to rest undisturbed in the oven until set, about 30 minutes longer. Transfer to a rack and let cool. Cover and chill overnight before serving.

Just before serving, run a knife around the pan sides to loosen the cake. Release the pan sides and place the cake on a plate. Arrange the whole berries evenly around the top, marking a slice with each berry.

Strawberry, White Chocolate, Mascarpone and Marsala Torte

This elegant yet easy dessert makes a showy finale to a dinner party or Easter celebration. It can be prepared with either the soft, small bakery style ladyfingers or the firmer, longer packaged variety.

1 1/3 cups chilled whipping cream
6 ounces good-quality white chocolate, chopped
1 pound to 18 ounces mascarpone cheese, room temperature

Four 3-ounce packages ladyfinger biscuits or 4 packages boudoir or champagne biscuits
1 cup (about) dry Marsala
1 1/2 pounds strawberries, hulled, quartered, sliced

12 white chocolate-dipped strawberries, optional

Combine 1/3 cup whipping cream and white chocolate in large metal bowl. Stir over saucepan of simmering water until chocolate is melted and smooth. Remove from heat; let stand until just cool to touch. Gradually stir in mascarpone. Let cool to room temperature.

Brush several ladyfingers generously with Marsala, and arrange decoratively, Marsala side up, in single layer over bottom of 10-inch-diameter spring form pan, trimming to fit if necessary. Arrange enough ladyfingers around edge of pan to cover (boudoir and champagne biscuits will need to be cut in half). Brush generously with Marsala.

Using electric hand mixer, beat cream in large bowl until soft peaks form. Fold cream into mascarpone mixture to form mousse. Spoon half of mousse over ladyfingers in pan. Sprinkle half of strawberries evenly over mousse.

Brush one side of remaining ladyfingers with Marsala. Arrange enough ladyfingers, Marsala side down, over berries to cover completely and evenly. Brush tops of ladyfingers with Marsala. Repeat layering with remaining mousse, berries and ladyfingers. Brush Marsala over final layer of ladyfingers. Cover with plastic wrap and refrigerate overnight.

TIP: Can be made up to 3 days ahead. Keep refrigerated. Run a small sharp knife around pan sides to loosen. Invert torte onto platter. Release pan sides and remove pan. Garnish with white chocolate-dipped strawberries and serve.

Stuffed Pastries

In the ranks of Italian filled sweet pastries the piconi marchigiani have a place of their own as dessert, breakfast food and treat for afternoon tea. In some versions the ricotta used for the filling is flavored with a little rum.

For Pastry
4 1/3 cups all-purpose flour
5 egg yolks, beaten
1 cup butter; softened
1 1/4 cups sugar
Grated zest of lemon

For Filling
3 egg yolks
1 1/4 cups sugar
Pinch of ground cinnamon
Grated zest of 1 lemon
1 cup rum
3 oz semisweet dark chocolate, grated
3 oz shelled almonds, ground
1 lb ricotta cheese

FOR PASTRY: Heap the flour on a board and make a well in the center. Put in the egg yolks, butter, sugar and a little lemon zest. Knead quickly to obtain medium-soft dough. Roll into a ball, wrap in plastic and chill for 1 hour.

FOR FILLING: In a bowl, beat the egg yolks (reserving a little for brushing the pastries), sugar, cinnamon, lemon zest, rum, chocolate and almonds into the ricotta. The mixture should be thick.

Roll the dough out thinly. Cut into 3 in circles. Put 1 teaspoon of the filling in the center of each circle and fold the dough over into a half-moon shape, pressing with your fingers to seal the edges well. Preheat the oven to 300 degrees F.

Put the pastries onto a buttered baking sheet and brush them with the reserved beaten egg. Bake in the oven until a toothpick inserted into one of them comes out dry, about 20 minutes.

Tiramisu

Literally translated *pick-me-up*, tiramisu appropriately lightens the mood at the end of any dinner party. Store-bought pound cake may be used instead of the ladyfingers, and instant espresso or very strong coffee will do if an espresso machine is not at hand.

5 extra-large egg yolks
5 tablespoons sugar
1 2/3 cups mascarpone cheese, chilled
1 3/4 cups heavy cream, chilled
1/4 cup brewed strong espresso, cooled
1/4 cup coffee-flavored liqueur
24 good-quality plain ladyfingers
Fresh raspberries, optional
Dutch-processed cocoa

Using an electric mixer, beat egg yolks and sugar in large bowl until pale yellow, smooth and shiny, about 7 minutes. Add the mascarpone cheese and beat until thickened and smooth, about 4 minutes. In another bowl, beat cream until soft peaks form. Using a rubber spatula or whisk, fold the whipped cream into the mascarpone mixture until thoroughly blended.

Combine espresso and liqueur in small bowl. Arrange the ladyfingers in a single layer over the bottom of a decorative 10 inch-diameter serving bowl. Brush some of the espresso mixture evenly over the ladyfingers. Turn the ladyfingers over and brush again until each one is almost soaked through with the espresso mixture. Arrange raspberries around the edge, if desired. Spoon some of the mascarpone mixture over the ladyfingers to make an even 1/2 inch-thick layer. Place the remaining ladyfingers in a single layer over the mascarpone mixture and brush their tops with the remaining espresso mixture. Again, arrange raspberries around the edge, if using. Spoon the remaining mascarpone mixture on top, smoothing to cover completely. Cover and chill at least 6 hours or up to 2 days before serving.

TO SERVE: Sift a light dusting of cocoa over the top. Using a large serving spoon, scoop portions of the tiramisu onto individual plates. *62*

Tiramisu with Marsala

Tiramisu, which means "pick me up" in Italian, uses espresso to help moisten and flavor the crisp ladyfinger cookie layers. Brandy, rum or Marsala is typically used to flavor the fluffy custard cream filling (also referred to as zabaglione). Here the Sicilian Marsala wins out, adding complexity to this superb version of the must-try Italian dessert.

Tip: Cocoa powder is wonderful sprinkled on cakes, chocolate truffles and tiramisu, but without the proper cook's tool, you end up with clumps or a cloud of dust. Use a fine mesh shaker to sprinkle the cocoa powder evenly over this dessert. The shaker is also great for sprinkling spices on food or for sifting flour.

1 cup plus 1 tablespoon sugar
2/3 cup sweet Marsala wine
8 large egg yolks
Three 8-ounce containers mascarpone cheese.
1/2 cup freshly brewed espresso mixed with 1/2 cup water or 1 cup very strong hot coffee (brewed from 1 1/4 cups water and 3/4 cup ground espresso beans)
1/4 cup Kahlua liqueur
200 grams (7ounces) Champagne biscuits (crisp ladyfingers cookies)
1 1/2 tablespoons unsweetened cocoa

Whisk 1 cup sugar, Marsala and yolks in medium metal bowl. Set bowl over saucepan of gently boiling water (do not allow bottom of bowl to touch water). Whisk constantly until candy thermometer registers 165 degrees F and mixture thickens, about 4 minutes. Remove bowl from over water. Gradually add mascarpone, whisking vigorously until well blended.

Combine espresso, Kahlua and remaining 1 tablespoon sugar in another medium bowl; stir until sugar dissolves. Completely submerge 1 biscuit into espresso mixture for 1 second; shake off excess liquid. Place biscuit in bottom of 13x9-inch oval gratin dish. Repeat with enough biscuits to just cover bottom of pan.

Spoon half of mascarpone mixture over biscuits, spreading to cover. Dip remaining biscuits one at a time into espresso mixture and arrange atop mascarpone mixture (discard remaining espresso mixture). Spoon remaining mascarpone mixture over biscuits, spreading to cover. Sift over, covering mascarpone mixture completely. Cover and refrigerate overnight.

DO-AHEAD TIP: Can be made 3 days ahead. Cover and keep refrigerated.

Cookies

Almond Brittle

This candy has been very popular for a long time, but this recipe is an Italian version using toasted almonds instead of the usual peanuts.

4 cups sliced almonds, toasted
3 cups granulated sugar
1/4 cup water

Use a teflon coated baking pan, or prepare a baking sheet by lightly spraying with oil spray in a heavy saucepan, combine the sugar and water and cook over medium high heat until the sugar has melted. Continue to cook until the mixture turns golden brown, about 15 to 20 minutes. Remove from the heat, and fold in the almonds immediately. Pour out onto the baking sheet, spreading to an even thickness. Cool completely, and then break into pieces. Store in an airtight container.

Anginetti

Often called Anginetti, or Ginetti, these buttery cookies are topped with a lemon flavored icing which is delicious. These cookies can be found under many different names, including Ginetti, or Anginetti. The cookie themselves are light and buttery, while the lemon flavored icing adds a nice contrast to the cookie itself.

1/2 cup granulated sugar
6 tablespoons unsalted butter
2 teaspoons vanilla extract
1 teaspoon grated lemon zest, finely chopped
3 large eggs
2 cups all-purpose flour
2 teaspoons baking powder
Icing
1 tablespoon unsalted butter
3 cups sifted confectioner's, or icing sugar
2 tablespoons water
2 tablespoons lemon juice
colored sprinkles (optional)

Preheat oven to 350 F. Line a baking sheet with silicon sheets, or parchment paper. In a large mixing bowl, beat together the sugar, vanilla, lemon peel and 6 tablespoons of butter with an electric mixer until well blended. Add the eggs one at a time, beating well after each addition. Continue to beat for 1 minute. Stir in flour and baking powder and blend just until mixed. The dough should be soft and sticky. Spoon dough into a pastry bag fitted with a 3/8-inch round tip. Pipe 2-inch diameter rings onto the prepared baking sheets. With wet fingertips, press the ends of each ring together to form a smooth ring. Bake about 20 minutes or until light golden brown.
To make the icing, melt 1 tablespoon of butter over low heat. Add the sugar, water, and lemon juice and whisk until the sugar melts and the mixture is heated through. If icing is too thick to brush easily, add more water to thin. Remove the cookies from the oven and immediately brush warm icing over the hot cookies. Sprinkle with colored sprinkle if using. Cool iced cookies for a few minutes, and then transfer them to wire racks to cool completely. Store in an airtight container.

Almond Biscotti

Biscotti means "twice-baked"; the first baking cooks the loaf of
cookie dough and the second baking dries out and crisps the
sliced cookies. Throughout Italy, an assortment of biscotti and
other sweets are traditionally served with a glass of Vin Santo or an
espresso or cappuccino for dipping.

1/2 cup unsalted butter, chilled
1 cup sugar
2 extra-large eggs, at room temperature
2 1/3 cups unbleached all-purpose flour
1 cup slivered blanched almonds, chopped
2 teaspoons minced lemon zest
2 teaspoons fresh lemon juice
2 1/4 teaspoons aniseeds
1 1/2 teaspoons baking powder
1/4 teaspoon salt
1 tablespoon vanilla extract
1 teaspoon almond extract

Preheat an oven to 375 degrees F. Line 2 baking sheets with
parchment (baking) paper.

In a mixing bowl, using an electric mixer set on medium speed,
beat together the butter and sugar until light and fluffy, 2-3
minutes. Beat in the eggs, one at a time, beating well after each
addition. Gradually add the flour, beating until well mixed. Then
add the almonds, lemon zest and juice, aniseeds, baking powder,
salt, and vanilla and almond extracts and continue to beat until
blended.

Shape the dough into 4 logs, each one about 2 inches wide and
3/4 inch high, and place on the prepared baking sheets. Place in
the center of the oven and immediately reduce the heat to 325
degrees F. Bake until light golden brown, puffy and a little firm
when pressed on top, 25-30 minutes.

Remove the baking sheets from the oven and immediately slice the logs crosswise on the sheets into pieces 1/2 inch thick. Separate the pieces on the sheets, keeping them upright and spacing them so that the air can circulate around them.

Reduce the oven temperature to 275 degrees F. Place the sheets in the center of the oven and bake until the biscotti are dry and crisp, 20-30 minutes. Transfer the biscotti to racks and let cool completely. Store in an airtight container.

Amaretti

Perfect for a light ending to a big meal, amaretti are puffy confections served frequently in Italy. A cup of espresso or cappuccino would be the perfect complement.

2 egg whites
1 1/4 cups blanched whole almonds
3/4 cup granulated sugar
1/4 teaspoon cream of tartar
1/4 teaspoon almond extract
1/4 cup slivered almonds

In a large mixing bowl let the egg whites stand at room temperature for 30 minutes. Meanwhile, line 2 cookie sheets with parchment paper or brown kraft paper. Set aside. In a food processor bowl or blender container process or blend whole almonds with 1/4 cup of the sugar till almonds are finely ground. Set aside.

Add the cream of tartar and almond extract to the egg whites. Beat with an electric mixer on medium speed till soft peaks form (tips curl). Gradually add the remaining 1/2 cup sugar, 1 tablespoon at a time, beating on high speed till very stiff peaks form (tips stand straight) and sugar is almost dissolved. Fold in ground almonds.

Drop meringue mixture by rounded teaspoons 1 1/2 inches apart onto the prepared cookie sheets. Sprinkle a few slivered almonds over each cookie. Bake in a preheated 300 degrees oven for 12 to 15 minutes, or till cookies just begin to brown (centers will be soft). Turn off oven. Let cookies dry in oven with the door closed for 30 minutes. Peel cookies from paper. Store in an airtight container in a cool, dry place for up to 1 week.

Biscotti

Biscotti are a traditional Italian treat often served with strong, hot coffee. The small, crisp slices are made for dunking. For a spiced version, omit the almond extract and stir in 1/2 teaspoon ground cinnamon, 1/4 teaspoon ground cloves, and 1/4 teaspoon ground nutmeg.

1 cup granulated sugar
1 teaspoon baking soda
1/4 teaspoon salt
3 eggs
1 teaspoon vanilla
1/2 teaspoon almond extract
2 3/4 cups all-purpose flour
1 cup finely chopped slivered almonds, walnuts, pecans, pine nuts,macadamia nuts, or hazelnuts
1 beaten egg
1 teaspoon water

In a large mixing bowl stir together the sugar, baking soda, and salt. Stir in 3 eggs, vanilla, and almond extract. Stir in the flour and chopped nuts. On a well-floured surface, knead dough 8 to 10 times. Divide in half. On a lightly floured surface shape each half into a log about 9 inches long. Place logs about 4 inches apart on a lightly greased cookie sheet. Pat each log into a flattened loaf about 10 inches long and 2 to 4 inches wide. Stir together the egg and water; brush over loaves.

Bake in a preheated 325 degrees F oven for 30 minutes. Cool on a rack. Cut each loaf diagonally into 2-inch-thick slices. Place slices, cut-sides down, on ungreased cookie sheets. Bake in the 325 degrees F oven for 5 minutes. Turn slices over and bake for 5 to 8 minutes more, or till dry and crisp. Remove cookies from pan and cool on a rack.

Biscuit Tortoni

Almond, rum, and chocolate in a smooth, creamy base. Great finale for a dinner party or cookout. To serve, spoon the biscuit tortoni into individual old-fashioned ice cream dishes or custard cups.

1/2 cup chopped blanched almonds

5 ounces amarettini cookies

3 tablespoons dark rum

3/4 cup semisweet chocolate chips

1 cup heavy cream, chilled

3 tablespoons brandy

1 quart vanilla

Preheat oven or toaster oven to 350 degrees F (175 degrees C).

Place chopped almonds on a tray and toast in preheated oven until lightly colored and fragrant, 5 to 8 minutes. Let cool completely.

Crumble the cookies into 1/2 inch pieces by wrapping in a tea towel and tapping lightly with a rolling pin or mallet. Do not crush into small pieces. Place crumbled cookies in a medium bowl and sprinkle with rum. Toss with almonds and chocolate chips. Set aside.

In a large bowl, beat cream with an electric mixer until thickened. Pour in brandy and beat until soft peaks form. Spoon whipped cream over cookie mixture. In whipped cream bowl, now beat ice cream just until softened (with a flat whip, if available). Fold cookie and cream mixture into ice cream. Freeze until serving.

Brutti Ma Buoni

This is yet another traditional cookie recipe that can be found in many variations across Italy.

Although delicious, these cookies are not suitable for making too far in advance, or for freezing. This variation uses chocolate in place of the usual chopped nuts.

4 large egg whites
1 cup sugar
3 tablespoons all-purpose flour
1 teaspoon vanilla
2 cups chopped dark (or semisweet) chocolate
icing sugar (optional)

Preheat oven to 350 degrees F. Line two baking sheets with parchment paper or silicon baking sheets. In a double boiler, or in a small pot placed in a larger pot with simmering water over low heat, cook the egg whites with the sugar, stirring often until the mixture is opaque. This will take about 10 minutes. Remove from the heat, and beat on high speed with an electric mixer until the mixture is thickened and glossy. Fold in the flour, extract and chocolate.

Drop by heaping teaspoonfuls about 2 inches apart onto prepared baking sheets. Baking one sheet at a time, bake 25 minutes, or until the cookies are light brown. Cool on wire racks. Sprinkle with icing sugar if using, and store in an airtight container.

Chocolate Biscotti

Although it would be unlikely to find biscotti served in a traditional pizzeria in the historic center of Naples, they are common in the pizzerias popular today. These delicious cookies are rich with chocolaty flavor and not too sweet and have the perfect consistency for dipping. The almonds add extra crunch.

1/4 cup whole blanched almonds
3 tablespoons unsalted butter, at room temperature
1/2 cup sugar
1 egg
1/2 teaspoon pure vanilla extract
3/4 cup all-purpose flour
1/4 cup sifted Dutch-process cocoa
1/2 teaspoon baking powder
1/8 teaspoon baking soda
2 oz semisweet chocolate or bittersweet chocolate, coarsely chopped

Preheat an oven to 400 degrees F. Spread the almonds in a single layer on a baking sheet. Place in the oven until lightly toasted and fragrant, about 7 minutes. Remove from the oven and let cool. Reduce the oven temperature to 350 degrees F.

Line the bottom of a large baking sheet with parchment (baking) paper or aluminum foil. Nest the paper-lined sheet in a second baking sheet of the same size; this will prevent the bottoms of the cookies from scorching.

In a large bowl, using a wooden spoon, cream together the butter and sugar until light and fluffy. Add the egg and vanilla and beat well. Set aside.

In a food processor fitted with the metal blade, combine the flour, cocoa, baking powder and baking soda. Pulse briefly to combine, and then add the chopped chocolate. Process continuously until the chocolate is finely and evenly chopped.

74

Add the flour mixture to the butter mixture and blend just until combined. The mixture should come together into soft dough. Add the almonds and mix until evenly distributed.

On a lightly floured work surface, use your hands to shape the dough into a log about 13 inches long and 2 1/2 inches in diameter. Place the log on the prepared baking sheet. Bake until the edges are firm (the center will not seem done yet), 30-35 minutes.

Remove from the oven and let cool until lukewarm, about 30 minutes. Reduce the oven temperature to 300 degrees F. Slice the log crosswise on a slight diagonal into pieces 3/4 inch (2 cm) wide and return to the baking sheet, cut sides down. Bake for 10 minutes. Turn the cookies over and bake until lightly toasted, about 10 minutes longer. Remove from the oven, transfer to a rack and let cool completely. Store in an airtight container for up to 1 month. The biscotti can actually be stored for up to 6 months, if you can keep your hands out of the container. If they have become soft, recrisp them in a 350 degree F. oven for 5-6 minutes.

Chocolate Coated Almonds

4 cups whole unbleached almonds
1 1/2 cups sugar
1/3 cup water
1/2 cup unsweetened cocoa, sifted

Preheat the oven to 400 degrees F. Spread the almonds out on a baking sheet and toast for 10 minutes, until lightly browned. Cool slightly.

In a medium heavy-bottomed saucepan, stir the sugar and water together with a wooden spoon. Bring the mixture to a boil, and cook until it turns clear, about 2 minutes. Add the cocoa, and stir well to dissolve. Add the nuts, and continue to stir constantly, turning the nuts oven in the mix. Cook for 3 to 4 minutes, until the sugar recrystallizes to a sandy texture that coats the nuts. Be careful not to overwork the nuts or the sugar will fall off. Pour the nuts out onto a baking sheet and spread to cool.

Pick the cooled nuts off the sheet to separate them from the excess sugar, and serve at room temperature. Store in a sealed plastic bag at room temperature.

Chocolate Meringue Cookies

These cookies are delicious, and store well for at least two weeks in an airtight container. I garnish half of my cookies with a light dusting of confectioner's sugar, and half with cocoa which makes a nice presentation on my cookie tray.

3 large egg whites
1/ 4 teaspoon cream of tartar
3/4 cup sugar
3 tablespoons unsweetened cocoa

For Garnish (optional)
powdered sugar or cocoa

Preheat the oven to 300 degrees F. Place the egg whites and cream of tartar in a bowl, and beat with an electric mixer until soft peaks form. Begin to add the sugar slowly, and continue to beat on high speed until the whites are stiff and shiny. Sift the cocoa over the egg whites, and fold gently until mixed. Drop the batter by the tablespoon onto parchment lined baking sheets. If you want to garnish them, then sift a small amount of the powdered sugar and/or cocoa on top of the cookies before baking. Bake for about 1 hour, or until the meringues are very dry. Cool, and then peel the cookies carefully from the parchment. Store in an airtight container until ready to serve.

Italian Lemon Drops

These lemon flavored little cookies are a great addition on a cookie tray, or with a cup of coffee. They are very easy to make, and freeze well although I would not frost them before freezing.

If using frozen cookies, frost them just before serving.

1 cup granulated sugar
1/2 cup shortening
6 eggs
1 teaspoon lemon extract
4 cups flour
1 teaspoon grated, chopped lemon zest
2 1/2 teaspoons baking powder
dash of salt

Icing
2 cups powdered sugar
fresh lemon juice

Preheat the oven to 350 degrees F. Either lightly grease two baking or cookie sheets, or use silicon sheets on them. In a large bowl, cream together the sugar and shortening. Add the eggs, lemon extract and grated lemon zest, and mix well. Stir together the flour, salt, and baking powder. Add this dry mixture to the bowl with the eggs and mix well. Roll the dough into small balls about 3/4 inch big, and place on the baking sheets at least 1 to 2 inches apart. Bake the cookies for 10 to 15 minutes. Cool on a wire rack.

In a medium bowl with an electric mixer, beat together the powdered sugar and a tablespoon or two of lemon juice. Only add as much lemon juice as is needed to make an icing that will coat the cookies. With a small spoon, drizzle the icing over the cookies, allowing it to run down the sides. Let sit out for an hour or two until set. Store in an airtight container.

Juliet's Kisses

In the Western world, the food with the most magical, famous, and elaborate history as an aphrodisiac is chocolate.

Shakespeare's balcony love scene between Romeo and Juliet may be the greatest romantic scene in the history of English literature. It sure has its fans. The story of the two lovers from feuding families has been bringing tourists to Number 23 Via Capello for hundreds of years.

2 large eggs, hard-boiled
8 ounces semisweet chocolate, chopped, melted
1/2 cup (1 stick) unsalted butter, room temperature
1 cup sugar
1 1/3 cups all-purpose flour, sifted
Powdered sugar

Preheat oven to 350 degrees F. Butter and flour large baking sheet. Discard the white of one of the eggs. Press the whole egg and egg yolk through fine strainer. Set aside.

Using electric mixer, beat butter and sugar in large bowl until light and fluffy. Add the melted chocolate and beat until smooth. Stir in the flour and eggs (dough will be firm).

Spoon the dough onto prepared baking sheet, forming smooth, 1-inch-wide mounds. Bake until cookies are puffed and cracked, about 18 minutes. Cool cookies completely. Dust with powdered sugar and serve.

Ginger-Pear Biscotti

This highly unique biscotti is redolent of ginger and flecked with dried pear. We like to eat it in the classic manner, dipped in port or another dessert wine.

Take care not to overcook these during the second baking. Remove them from the oven as soon as the cookies are very dry to the touch and slightly crisp; like all biscotti, they will continue to crisp with cooling. For more brittle biscotti, lay the cookies on their sides rather than standing them upright during the second baking.

3 cups all-purpose flour
1/2 tablespoon baking powder
2 teaspoons ground ginger
1/4 teaspoon salt
2/3 cup granulated sugar
6 ounces dried pears, diced (about 3/4 cup)
4 large eggs
1/2 tablespoon vanilla extract
1/3 cup honey

Preheat the oven to 350 degrees F. Line a 12-by-15 inch baking sheet with baker's parchment.

Sift the flour, baking powder, ginger, salt, and sugar together into a large mixing bowl. Mix in the dried pears and make a well in the center.

Whisk the eggs in a small bowl. Add the vanilla and honey, whisking until well blended. Pour into the well of the flour mixture. Stir with a wooden spoon until the flour is completely incorporated. Set aside for 5 minutes.

Divide the dough in half and form each half on the prepared baking sheet into a 3/4-inch-high loaf about 10 inches long and 3 inches wide. Bake for about 30 minutes, until golden.

Remove the loaves to a work surface. With a serrated knife, cut into 1/2-inch-thick diagonal slices. For brittle biscotti, lay the slices on their sides on the baking sheet. Return to the oven and toast for about 10 minutes, until lightly browned. For slightly softer biscotti, stand the slices upright and toast for about 15 minutes.

Remove the biscotti to a wire rack and cool completely.

Mascarpone Fig Jam Cookies

Mascarpone cheese makes these cookies very tender, and the fig jam adds a delicious sweetness.

These cookies store well for up to two weeks refrigerated, and freeze well for up to two months in an airtight container.

1/2 cup or 1 stick unsalted butter, brought to room temperature
1 1/2 cups sugar
1 large egg
1 teaspoon vanilla extract
1/2 cup softened Mascarpone cheese
2 3/4 cups all-purpose flour
1/2 teaspoon baking powder
1/2 teaspoon salt
1 cup fig jam, or jam of choice

Beat together the butter and sugar until light. Add the egg and vanilla, and mix until smooth. Add the mascarpone cheese, and beat until smooth. Sift together the dry ingredients, and fold them into the butter mixture, mixing just until combined. Wrap the dough in plastic wrap, and refrigerate 1 hour. Preheat oven to 325 degrees F. Place sheets of parchment paper, or silicone baking liners on two cookie pans.

On a lightly floured counter or board, roll the dough into 1/2 inch balls.

Using a blunt round object like the end of a wooden spoon, create an indentation in the center of each cookie. Place the cookies 2 inches apart, and bake for 12 to 15 minutes, or just as the cookies begin to color. While still warm, use the spoon to redefine the circle, and then carefully spoon a little jam into each cookie. Let sit at room temperature until the jam is set. Store in an airtight container.

Mostaccioli

Mostaccioli are cookies created from a dense, honey flavored dough that encases a chocolate, almond filling. This traditional Calabrian specialty is a great addition to any cookie tray.

2 pounds lightly toasted almonds
2 pounds honey
1 (350gm) package chocolate chips
4 egg yolks
6-8 cups all-purpose flour
1 tablespoon baking powder

Melt the chocolate chips in a double boiler with 1/4 cup of the honey until melted. Mix the almonds into this mixture and set aside to cool slightly. Preheat the oven to 300 degrees F. Make a mound of 6 cups of the flour on a pastry board or the counter, add the baking powder, and create a well in the center. Add the egg yolks and using a fork, mix into the flour. Begin to add the honey into this well, using a fork to combine with the flour. Continue to use all the honey, adding more flour as needed. Knead the dough until smooth.

Divide the dough into 5 equal pieces. Roll each into a ball, and then flatten into a 1 inch thick oval. At one long end of the oval, place a few teaspoons of the chocolate mixture, and then fold over the other side to close it in. Place theses loaves on a lightly floured cookie sheet. Bake for about 30-40 minutes until golden brown. Cool completely and slice into 1/2 inch slices.

Red Wine Biscuits

These savory biscuits or cookies are great with a glass of wine
before dinner, or after dinner with a selection of Italian cheese and
a glass of robust red wine.

2 1/2 cups all-purpose flour
1/2 cup sugar
1 1/2 teaspoon baking powder
1/2 teaspoon salt
1 teaspoon cracked black pepper
1/2 cup dry red wine
1/2 cup live oil
1 egg white
2 tablespoons sesame seeds

Preheat oven to 350 degrees F. Mix together the flour, sugar,
baking powder, salt and pepper. Add the wine and olive oil, and
mix together until smooth. Divide the dough into three pieces,
and shape each into a log shape, about 2 inches across. Beat the
egg white until foamy, and brush the tops of the three logs.
Sprinkle with the sesame seeds. Cut the logs with a sharp knife
into 3/4 inch slices. Place these slices 1 inch apart on lightly
greased and floured baking sheets. Bake for 25 minutes until
lightly browned. Cool on wire racks, and store in an airtight
container.

Raisin Cookies

These cookies are great with a cup of coffee for a mid-morning snack. You can double the recipe and freeze half, and just defrost the second batch when needed.

1 cup water
1 cup raisins
1 cup shortening
3 eggs
1/2 teaspoon salt
1 cup sugar
1 1/2 teaspoons cinnamon
3 1/2 cups flour
3 teaspoons baking powder

Preheat the oven to 350 degrees F. and lightly grease two baking sheets. Place the water and raisins in a small pot, and bring to a boil. Add the shortening, and remove from the heat, stirring until the shortening has melted. In a bowl, beat together the eggs and the sugar until light. Add the raisin mixture to the egg mixture, and then add the flour, salt, baking powder and cinnamon. Mix just until combined. Drop by tablespoons onto the prepared cookie sheets, leaving space between each cookie. Bake for 15 to 20 minutes, or until the cookies are set, and the bottoms lightly browned.

Ricotta Cheese Cookies

These are a tasty cookie made with ricotta cheese. They are brushed with a powdered sugar glaze.

2 sticks of butter at room temperature
2 cups of sugar
1 (15 oz) container ricotta cheese
2 teaspoons vanilla extract
dash of salt
1 teaspoon baking soda
1 teaspoon finely chopped lemon zest
4 cups all-purpose flour

Glaze

1 cup powdered sugar
milk
colored sprinkles

Preheat oven to 350 degrees F. Mix all the ingredients together until combined. The dough will be moist. Drop by a teaspoon onto a greased cookie sheet. Bake for about 10 minutes until firm. The cookies will be golden on the bottom, but will remain white on top.

Mix in enough milk to make a glaze that can be brushed. Lightly coat the tops of each cookie with the glaze and sprinkle with the colored sprinkles. Let dry fully before storing.

Romeo's Kisses

Baci di Romeo are small almond flavored cookies are
sandwiched together in pairs with chocolate filling. Paired with
Juliet's Kisses, they make a great addition to any cookie tray.

1/2 pound, or 2 sticks unsalted butter, softened
1/2 cup icing or confectioner's sugar
1/4 teaspoon salt
1/2 teaspoon almond extract
2 cups all-purpose flour

Filling
2 ounces semisweet or dark chocolate
2 tablespoons unsalted butter

1/3 cup toasted almonds ground
Preheat the oven to 350 degrees F. and prepare two baking sheets
either with silicon sheets, or by buttering them. In a large bowl,
beat together the butter and sugar until light and fluffy. Add the
salt and almond extract, and mix until smooth. Add the flour to
the bowl, and mix just until blended. Shape the cookies by rolling
small pieces of dough into 1 inch balls, and placing these one inch
apart on the baking sheets. Continue shaping the cookies in this
manner until you have used all of the dough. Bake the cookies
until firm, about 10 to 12 minutes. Do not let the cookies brown, or
they will dry out. Transfer to wire racks to cool.
To make the filling, melt the chocolate together with the butter in
a double boiler, or in a small pot set over a larger one half filled
with simmering water. Once the chocolate is melted and smooth,
mix in the ground almonds. Spread a small bit of icing (about 1
teaspoon full) unto the flat side of one cookie, and place another
cookie bottom side down onto the filling. Lightly press the cookies
together, and set back onto the wire racks until the chocolate has
set. Repeat this step until all of the cookies have been sandwiched
together with the filling.

Note: To toast the almonds, place them on a cookie sheet, and
bake for about 8 minutes or just until they begin to brown.

Sesame Seed Cookies

Biscotti Regina, are yet another traditional cookie now popular across Italy that originated in Sicily. Light, with a subtle flavor of orange, these cookies are nice with a cup of coffee, or on a holiday cookie tray.

4 cups all-purpose flour
1 cup sugar
1 tablespoon baking powder
dash of salt
1/2 pound (2 sticks) unsalted butter, softened
2 large eggs
1 teaspoon vanilla extract
1 teaspoon orange zest, finely chopped
1 1/2 cups fresh sesame seeds

Preheat the oven to 375 degrees F. Butter two baking sheets, or place silicon baking sheets on them. In a large bowl, stir together the flour, sugar, baking powder and salt. With an electric mixer on low speed, add the butter until blended. Whisk together the eggs, zest and vanilla, and add this to the flour mixture, and continue beating on low until you have a smooth dough. Pinch off a small piece of dough about the size of a small golf ball and roll it into a log about 2 inches long. Roll the log into the sesame seeds, pressing them lightly to stick. Place the cookie on the prepared baking sheets, and continue forming the remaining cookies the same way, keeping the cookies two inches apart. Bake for 25 minutes or until lightly browned. Cool, and store in airtight containers.

Sicilian Spiced Fig Cookies

Cuccidati are a traditional cookie very popular in southern Italy, particularly in Sicily. You can use either light or dark figs, but choose dried figs that are moist and tender.

Almonds can be substituted for the walnuts, but I prefer black walnuts as they have a rich nutty flavor. I also like to add a little chopped chocolate to the filling which gives sweetness to the cookie. To complete the cookie, you can either use an egg wash before baking, with colored sprinkles, or simply dust with confectioner's sugar before serving. These cookies keep well in an airtight tin for two to three weeks.

Dough

2 1/2 cups all-purpose flour
1/2 cup sugar
2 teaspoons baking powder
1/2 teaspoon salt
6 tablespoons unsalted, soft butter (about 3/4 of a stick)
2 large eggs
1 teaspoon vanilla extract

Filling

2 cups moist dried figs
1/2 cup raisins
1 cup walnuts, toasted and chopped
1/2 cup dark chocolate, chopped
1/3 cup honey
1/3 cup orange juice
1 teaspoon cinnamon
1/4 teaspoon nutmeg
1/4 teaspoon cloves
1 teaspoon orange zest, finely chopped

To Complete
confectioner's sugar

To prepare the dough, place the figs, raisins and chocolate in a food processor and pulse until finely chopped. Add the walnuts and pulse briefly again. Transfer to a bowl, and add the remaining filling ingredients. Stir well and set aside while you make the dough.

To make the dough, combine the flour, sugar, baking powder and salt in a large bowl. Cut the butter into the flour mixture until the mixture becomes pea sized pieces. Whisk together the eggs and vanilla, and mix this into the flour mixture. Knead very briefly to create a smooth dough, adding a little ice water if the dough is too dry to work. Bring the dough into a ball, wrap in plastic wrap, and refrigerate for 1 hour.

Preheat the oven to 350 degrees F. Butter two baking sheets, or cover with silicon sheets. Cut the dough into 6 equal sized pieces, and place one on a lightly floured surface. Roll this dough into a 9 X 5 inch rectangle. Trim the edges with a sharp knife, and spoon a strip of filling down the center about 1 inch in width. Lightly wet the edges of the dough with water, and then close, by folding one edge over the filling, and then the other, pressing the edges to seal. Roll the log over on the seam, and cut it into 3 pieces. With a sharp knife, make three slits into one side of each piece, about 3/4 inches long. Curve the pieces to open the slits and reveal the filling, and place the cookies on a baking sheet about 1 inch apart. Continue using up the remaining dough in this manner. Bake for about 25 minutes, or until the cookies are lightly browned. Cool, and lightly dust with the icing sugar before serving. Store in airtight containers.

Taralli

There are as many variations of Taralli, the traditional southern Italian ring cookie as there are families in Italy. Most recipes are shaped into a circle, and are topped with a simple icing as are these cookies are.

This variation of mine is quite simple, and is topped with a light lemon flavored icing. Although the cookies may seem a little dry and hard when they are first baked, they will soften up overnight. I prefer a very light icing, so I keep the mixture quite thin. If you prefer a thicker coating, just add a little less liquid.

5 1/2 cups all-purpose flour
1 1/2 tablespoon baking powder
6 eggs
1 1/2 sticks (about 12 tablespoons) of unsalted butter, melted
1 cup granulated sugar
1 1/2 tablespoons vanilla or lemon extract

Icing

3 cups icing or confectioner's sugar
2 tablespoons lemon juice
water
colored sprinkles

Line two baking or cookie sheets with parchment paper, and preheat the oven to 350 degrees F. Mix together the flour and baking powder in a bowl. In a separate bowl, whisk the eggs well, and then add the sugar. Mix well, and then add the melted butter and extract. Stir well until all the wet ingredients are well blended. Fold the dry ingredients into the wet and stir just until combined. Place the mixture on a lightly floured board or counter, and knead a minute or two until you have smooth dough. Divide the dough into about 30 equal pieces. Roll each piece by hand into a 5 inch rope. Pinch the ends together to make a circle. Place the cookies on the prepared baking sheets and bake for about 20 minutes, or until lightly browned and puffed. Cool to room temperature.

To make the icing, place the icing sugar in a bowl, and add the lemon juice. Slowly, begin to add a little water until you have the consistency you desire. Pick up each cookie, and dip them into the icing half way. Let the excess drip off, and then place the cookies on a rack or the paper you used to cook them on. If using the colored sprinkles, add them while the icing is still wet. Let the cookies dry completely, and then store them in an airtight container.

Tuscan Almond Cookies

In Tuscany these are the obligatory ending to any lunch. Small, dense-textured and dry, they are served with Vin Santo, a sweet and strongly perfumed wine made from grapes that have been left to dry in the cellars. The custom is to dip the cookies in the Vin Santo. The recipe is very simple, and the cookies will keep in an airtight container for several months.

8 2/3 cups all-purpose flour
8 eggs, beaten
5 cups superfine sugar
1/2 teaspoon baking soda
Salt
8 oz blanched almonds, finely chopped

Preheat the oven to 300 degrees F. Heap the flour in a mound on a pastry board. Make a well in the center and add the eggs, sugar, baking soda and a pinch of salt. Knead briefly. Add the almonds and knead again to mix thoroughly.

Roll the dough into lengths about 1 1/2 inches in diameter (2 in long). Flatten slightly. Arrange the cookies on a buttered and floured baking sheet.

Bake in the oven for 7 to 8 minutes, or until golden. Remove from the oven, cut into diagonal slices about 3/8 inch thick. Return to the oven to finish cooking until perfectly browned, about 7 to 10 minutes.

Fried Desserts

Cannoli

Cannoli are basically crisp, sweet crunchy tubes which are filled with a cream or ricotta cheese filling, often flavored with cocoa, nuts, chocolate, or candied fruits. This is a very traditional recipe for cannoli which are a very popular sweet in Sicily. You will need 3 to 4 metal cannoli tubes to makes these cannoli which are readily available at most kitchen stores. Do not fill the cannoli too far in advance, or they may become soggy.

Shells

2 cups all-purpose flour
2 tablespoons unsalted butter or shortening
1 teaspoon sugar
dash of salt
3/4 cup Marsala wine
1 egg white
vegetable oil for frying

Filling

3 cups full fat ricotta cheese
1/2 cup powdered sugar
1/2 cup mini chocolate chips, or coarsely grated chocolate
1/2 teaspoon vanilla extract
6 tablespoons mixed candies peel

Optional- 6 glaced cherries, finely chopped

To make the shells, mix together the flour, butter or shortening, sugar, and salt. Begin to add the wine, adding enough so that you have formed fairly firm dough. Knead for a few minutes until smooth. Form into a ball, wrap in plastic wrap, and let sit at room temperature for one hour. Cut the dough in half, and roll thinly to about a 1/4 inch thickness. Cut into 4 square. Place a metal diagonally across each square, and wrap the dough around the tube. Seal the edges with a little beaten egg white.

95

Heat the oil in a large pan until it reaches a temperature of 375 degrees F. Drop one or two tubes into the hot oil at one time, and cook until golden.

Remove from the pan, cool, and gently slide the cannoli shell from the tube. Continue to make the rest of the shells in this manner.

To make the filling, first let the ricotta sit in a strainer over a small bowl in the refrigerator for 30 minutes to remove excess water. Mix the ricotta with the rest of the ingredients. Chill in the refrigerator for at least 30 minutes. Fill each cannoli shell carefully, and sprinkle with a little extra powdered sugar if desired. Chill until you are ready to serve.

Cenci

Fried Bow Ties - Fried pastries of this type can be found across Italy, particularly during the carnival season. Cenci means tatters, which is what these pastries look like before you fry them. They are great warm or at room temperature, but must be eaten the same day.

1 cup all-purpose flour
3 tablespoons melted butter
2 tablespoons granulated sugar
1 egg
2 tablespoons Vin Santo wine or rum
1 teaspoon vanilla extract
pinch of salt
oil for deep frying
confectioners sugar

In a medium sized bowl, place the flour and slowly add the other ingredients mixing well. Form into dough, and lightly knead for a minute or two. Cover with plastic wrap and let sit for an hour. Roll out onto a lightly floured surface until very thin. Cut into strips about 6-8 inches long and 1/2 inch wide, and gently tie into a knot. Fry in oil heated to 375 degrees F. until golden. Place on a plate covered with paper towels, and lightly dust with confectioner's sugar.

Rice Fritters

These light rice fritters are very popular, especially during Carnivale. I use a light oil for frying as I find olive oil adds too much of it's own flavor to these delicate tasting fritters.

4 cups milk
6 tablespoons granulated sugar
2 tablespoons sweet butter
grated zest of 1 lemon
1 teaspoons vanilla extract
1 1/2 cups of Arborio rice
2 eggs, separated
5 cups of oil for frying

Combine the milk, sugar, butter, vanilla and lemon zest in a medium sized pot and bring to a boil. Reduce the heat to simmer and cook, stirring occasionally until the rice is tender and the milk is absorbed. Let cool to room temperature.

Add the egg yolks and mix well. Whip the egg whites until stiff peaks form, and fold into the rice mixture. In a heavy pot, fry in oil that has been heated to 375 degrees F. until golden brown. It takes only a few minutes, so watch carefully. Remove to a plate covered with paper towels to absorb the oil. Sprinkle with a little more granulated sugar, and serve warm.

Rocotta Fritters

8 oz. ricotta cheese
2 eggs
1/3 cup flour
1-1/2 tablespoon butter, softened
1 tablespoon grated lemon zest
Pinch of salt
Vegetable oil for frying
Honey for drizzling

In a bowl, combine the ricotta cheese with eggs. Add the flour and blend well.

Add the butter, lemon zest, and salt. Beat until all ingredients are well blended.

Allow the batter to rest for 1 hour.

In a frying pan over medium-high heat, add oil to a depth of 1/2-inch. When oil is hot, add batter, 1 TB. at a time, allowing fritters to fry without crowding.

When fritters become a light golden brown, turn them over. Transfer fritters to a paper-towel covered plate to drain. Place fritters on a serving platter and drizzle with honey. Best served warm.

Struffoli

6 egg yolks
zest of 1 lemon
1 tablespoon vanilla extract, or flavored liqueur of choice
3 cups all-purpose flour
pinch of salt
oil for frying
2 cups honey
juice of 1 lemon

To Garnish

Candied Sprinkles or Powdered Sugar

In a large bowl, combine flour, egg yolks, zest, salt, and vanilla. Knead to form a firm dough, about 8-10 minutes. Cover with plastic wrap and refrigerate for 30 minutes. To shape, pinch off small pieces and roll into logs about the width of your finger. Cut these logs into 1/2 inch pieces and roll each into a ball shape. Continue shaping in this manner until you have used up all your dough. Heat your oil to 375 degrees F in a heavy pot, and fry 6 or so balls at a time until golden brown. Drain on paper towels.

Once all your struffoli are cooked, heat the honey with the lemon juice in a wide saucepan. Add the struffoli and carefully stir until the struffoli are well coated. Cool 5 minutes and then place on a large platter in the shape of a pyramid or a ring. Sprinkle with the candies sprinkles or powdered sugar and serve.

Pasticitti

4 cups all-purpose flour

2 teaspoons baking powder

1 pinch salt

1 cup white sugar

1 cup margarine

2 eggs

1/2 cup milk

2 teaspoons vanilla extract

6 tablespoons cornstarch

3/4 cup white sugar

4 egg yolks, divided

1 quart milk, room temperature

1 tablespoon butter or margarine

1 teaspoon vanilla extract

2 tablespoons confectioners' sugar for dusting

In a large bowl, stir together the flour, baking powder, salt and 1 cup of sugar. Cut in margarine by pinching between your fingers, or using a pastry blender, until the mixture has lumps no larger than small peas. Make a well in the center, and pour in the eggs, 1/2 cup milk and 2 teaspoons vanilla. Stir until the mixture comes together, and then knead for about 5 turns on a lightly floured surface.

Roll out the dough to about 1/4 inch thickness. Grease two 12 cup muffin tins or tart pans. Cut out 20 circles using a 3 inch cookie cutter or drinking glass. Line the muffin cups with the dough. Set aside the remaining dough to cut out tops for the cups.

In the top of a double boiler, or in a metal bowl set atop a saucepan of simmering water, whisk together the cornstarch and 3/4 cup sugar. Gradually whisk in 3 of the egg yolks, and 1quart milk. Heat, stirring constantly, until thick and bubbling.

Remove from the heat, and stir in the butter and 1 teaspoon of vanilla until the butter is melted.

Preheat the oven to 350 degrees F (175 degrees C). Fill the pastry shells half way with the vanilla cream. Roll out remaining dough, and cut into circles for lids. Place over the top of the pastry shells, and seal the edges by pressing with the tines of a fork. Whisk the remaining egg yolk with a fork, and brush the tops of the pastry cups.

Bake for 25 minutes in the preheated oven, or until golden brown. Let cool in the tins before carefully loosening the edges to remove. Dust with confectioners' sugar before serving.

Zeppole

These fried, tender pastry rings can be dusted with sugar or drizzled with honey before serving. It is said that actually San Guiseppe, March 19th. is the day for zeppole, but they have become a very popular holiday food throughout the year. There are many variations to this recipe, some using a simple dough made of white wine and water while others use a liqueur to flavor, or eggs to lighten the dough. I personally like this recipe as it creates light airy zeppole that are really delicious. You can roll them in a cinnamon sugar mixture, powdered sugar, or coat them in honey.

2 cups all-purpose flour
1 cup melted butter
1 1/4 cup granulated sugar
4 egg yolks
pinch of salt
1/4 cup Vin Santo wine, rum, or Marsala wine
1 teaspoon vanilla extract
2 cups hot water
oil for deep frying

Topping

confectioners sugar, honey or granulated sugar with cinnamon

In a medium sized pot, place the water and butter, and heat until boiling. Add the flour, and mix well over the heat for few minutes, or until the mixture dries and begins to pull away from the pan. This may take anywhere from two to five minutes. Remove from the heat, and then slowly add the other ingredients mixing well. Form into a dough, and lightly knead for 5 minutes or so until satiny. Cover with plastic wrap and let sit for 30 minutes.

Divide the dough into three parts and break off small pieces and roll into a thickness about the width of your finger, 8 inches long. Fry in oil heated to 375 degrees F. until golden. Place on a plate covered with paper towels, and lightly dust with confectioner's sugar, sugar and cinnamon or melted honey. **103**

Zuccotto

This is a wonderful dessert that is a spectacular chocolate covered dome perfect for holidays or special occasions. Tender sponge cake is filled with a mixture made with whipped cream, chocolate, hazelnuts, and raspberries. Although it does sound very involved, if you make the dessert over a couple of days, it isn't that bad at all. The reaction of your guests will be well worth the effort it takes.

1 sponge cake

1/2 cup hazelnuts
1/2 cup sugar
1/4 cup water
1/4 cup liqueur of choice (raspberry works well)
2 cups heavy cream
1/4 cup icing sugar
4 ounces dark chocolate, coarsely chopped
1 pint raspberries (plus extra to decorate)

chocolate icing

9 ounces dark or semisweet chocolate
1 1/2 cups heavy cream

Toast the hazelnuts on a baking sheet, in a 350 degree F. oven for 10 minutes. Remove from the oven, and place in a kitchen towel. Rub the nuts inside the towel to remove their skins. Coarsely chop, and set aside.

Mix together the water, 1/2 cup sugar, and liqueur in a small pot. Bring to a boil, and stir until the sugar is dissolved. Remove from the heat and cool.

Line a deep bowl that is 9 inch in diameter, and 5 inches deep with plastic wrap. Cut the rectangular sponge cake into 9 squares, and then cut each square in half diagonally, creating 19 pieces of sponge cake in total.

104

Brush both sides of the sponge cake with the liqueur mixture, and fit them together in the lined bowl so the mold is completely lined. If you have any spaces visible, use spare pieces of the sponge cake moistened with the syrup to fill in the holes. Trim the top edge of the bowl evenly, and place it in the refrigerator while you prepare the filling.

Place the 2 cups of heavy cream with the icing sugar in a bowl, and beat with an electric mixer until the cream is in stiff peaks. Carefully fold in the hazelnuts, chopped chocolate and raspberries. Remove the mold from the refrigerator, and spoon the filling into the lined mold. Place the round cake on top of the filling, cover everything with plastic wrap, and refrigerate 12 hours.

Chop the chocolate finely, and place it in a bowl. Cook the cream until bubbly, and then pour it over the chocolate mixture. Let this mixture sit for 5 minutes, and then stir it until it is smooth. Leave sitting at room temperature. It will get thicker as it sits, but you need a mixture that is spreadable, but thick enough to nicely coat the bottom of the mold.

Remove the plastic wrap, place the cake on a wire rack top side down so the rounded end is on top, and remove the bowl. Place the wire rack over a baking sheet to catch the drips. Using a ladle, spoon the chocolate icing or ganache over the cake coating the entire surface. Decorate with extra hazelnuts and raspberries and serve.

Frozen Desserts

Basic Gelato

This recipe may be used as a base for your favorite flavors. Try adding vanilla, shaved chocolate or your favorite fruits.

2 cups milk

1 cup heavy cream

4 egg yolks

1/2 cup sugar

In a medium saucepan, mix milk and cream. Warm until foam forms around the edges. Remove from heat.

In a large bowl, beat the egg yolks and sugar until frothy. Gradually pour the warm milk into the egg yolks, whisking constantly. Return mixture to saucepan; cook over medium heat, stirring with a wooden spoon until the mixture gels slightly and coats the back of the spoon. If small egg lumps begin to show, remove from heat immediately.

Pour the mixture through a sieve or fine strainer into a bowl. Cover, and chill for several hours or overnight.

Pour the mixture into an ice cream maker, and freeze according to the manufacturer's instructions. Transfer to a sealed container, and freeze until firm. If the gelato is too firm, place it in the refrigerator until it reaches the desired consistency.

Cappuccino Gelato

The Saracens are credited with introducing ice cream to the Italians, who have made Italian gelato world famous. If you'd like this gelato to have a milder coffee flavor, make it with the mixture of espresso and liqueur known as caffè corretto. The addition of both white and bittersweet chocolate, although optional, is irresistible.

1 1/2 cups milk
1/2 cup light cream
1/4 cup sugar
4 extra-large egg yolks
2 teaspoons vanilla extract
2 tablespoons instant espresso coffee powder dissolved in 1 tablespoon milk, or 3 tablespoons brewed espresso mixed with 1 tablespoon coffee-flavored liqueur
1 oz white or bittersweet chocolate pieces, or a mixture, optional
Espresso-roast coffee beans or edible flowers, optional

In a saucepan over medium heat, combine the milk, cream and sugar and stir to dissolve the sugar. Bring almost to a boil (190 degrees F.), then remove from the heat. In a small bowl, stir together the egg yolks until blended. Stir a few tablespoons of the hot milk into the yolks. Then slowly pour the yolks into the hot milk, stirring constantly. Place over low heat and cook, stirring, until thickened, 1-2 minutes. Do not allow to boil. Immediately pour the mixture through a fine-mesh sieve into a bowl to remove any lumps. Stir in the vanilla and one of the espresso mixtures. Let cool, cover and chill well, at least 2 hours.

If desired, stir in the chocolate pieces, and then transfer to an ice cream maker. Freeze according to manufacturer's instructions.

Cappuccino Ice

In this day of complex appliances, it is good to be reminded that delicious desserts can be made with just a bowl and a whisk. It is just this type of quick-to-assemble granita that can be tended to easily in between the more demanding culinary tasks in a pizzeria. For a special treat, accompany the ice with chocolate biscotti.

2 1/2 cups hot brewed espresso or brewed French- or Italian-roast coffee
5-6 tablespoons sugar
1/2 cup half and half or milk
Unsweetened whipped cream
Chocolate shavings

In a 2 1/2-quart stainless-steel bowl, combine the hot espresso or coffee and 5 tablespoons sugar and stir until the sugar is completely dissolved. Add the half-and-half or milk and mix well. Taste and add the remaining 1 tablespoon sugar if desired. Refrigerate until cold, then place, uncovered, in the freezer.

When ice crystals have started to form around the edges, after 30-40 minutes, whisk the mixture vigorously to blend in the crystals. Return the bowl to the freezer and whisk again every 20-30 minutes until the mixture is a mass of coarse ice crystals yet still soft enough to spoon, 2-3 hours total. (If you forget the granita in the freezer and it hardens too much, let stand at room temperature for a few minutes, and then whisk it to the correct consistency.)

TO SERVE: Divide the ice among small serving bowls. Top each serving with a dollop of whipped cream and some chocolate shavings.

Crème Brulee Gelato

The popular decadent dessert is the inspiration behind this
equally rich gelato, which offers a denser, smoother texture than
traditional ice cream and better simulates the original custard. To
add the contrasting look and taste of a caramelized sugar topping
found in crème brulee, a crunchy caramel is swirled throughout,
and some is sprinkled on top. Spoon the gelato into a large soufflé
dish or individual crème brulee ramekins to replicate the
customary presentation.

For Ice Cream

2/3 cup sugar
8 large egg yolks
1/2 cup light corn syrup
3 1/2 cups half and half

For Caramel Crunch

1 tablespoon butter
1 cup sugar
1/4 cup water
1/2 teaspoon baking soda

FOR ICE CREAM: Stir sugar, egg yolks and corn syrup in
medium bowl to blend. Bring half-and-half just to a simmer in
heavy medium saucepan. Gradually stir half-and-half into yolk
mixture. Return mixture to saucepan.

Using wooden or rubber spatula, stir mixture over medium-low
heat until custard thickens and leaves path on back of spatula
when finger is drawn across, about 10 minutes (do not boil). Strain
through fine-mesh sieve if necessary. Transfer custard to bowl.
Cover and refrigerate until cold.

Process cold custard in ice cream maker according to
manufacturer's instructions. Transfer gelato to large soufflé dish
and freeze until almost firm.

MEANWHILE, PREPARE CARAMEL CRUNCH: Line baking sheet with foil; generously butter foil. Stir 1 cup sugar and water in heavy medium saucepan over medium-low heat until sugar dissolves. Increase heat and boil without stirring until amber color, brushing down sides of pan with wet pastry brush and swirling pan occasionally, about 10 minutes. Remove from heat. Stir in baking soda. Immediately transfer caramel mixture to buttered baking sheet. Allow caramel to cool completely.

Transfer caramel to plastic bag. Break caramel into small pieces. Swirl in all but 3/4 cup caramel pieces. Freeze until gelato is firm, about 4 hours. Sprinkle reserved 1/2 cup caramel pieces over gelato and serve.

Espresso Chip Gelato

Spoon this ice cream into espresso cups or coffee cups and top with whipped cream for a fun, unique finale to a light meal or as a midday pick-me-up.

1 1/4 cups sugar
8 large egg yolks
1/3 cup light corn syrup
3 cups whole milk
1/2 cup whipping cream
5 tablespoons instant coffee powder
8 ounces bittersweet or semisweet chocolate, chopped

Stir sugar, egg yolks and corn syrup in medium bowl to blend. Combine milk, cream and coffee powder in heavy medium saucepan. Bring milk mixture just to a simmer. Gradually stir milk mixture into yolk mixture. Return mixture to saucepan.

Using wooden or rubber spatula, stir mixture over medium-low heat until custard thickens and leaves path on back of spatula when finger is drawn across, about 10 minutes (do not boil). Strain through fine-mesh sieve if necessary. Transfer custard to bowl. Cover and refrigerate until cold.

Process custard in ice cream maker according to manufacturer's instructions. Mix in chopped chocolate. Transfer ice cream to container and freeze. Scoop ice cream into bowl and serve.

Espresso Granita

This light, refreshing dessert is perfect finish after a full meal on a hot summer day. This light, refreshing dessert is perfect finish after a full meal on a hot summer day.

4 cups cold espresso
1 1/2 cups superfine sugar

Heat the coffee and sugar together, until the sugar has completely dissolved. Pour this mixture into a shallow baking dish and freeze. After 30 minutes or so, stir to break up the ice crystals. Return the pan to the freezer and repeat this step until the mixture has frozen into a slush. It generally takes about 6 hours for this to take place. Serve immediately!

Lemon and Rosemary Granita

An icy treat for a warm summer evening, this granita gets an unexpected boost from the bold flavor of rosemary. You can put the hot lemon mixture directly into the freezer rather than chilling it first, but the freezing time will be longer.

3 cups water
1 cup plus 2 tablespoons sugar
4 4-inch sprigs fresh rosemary, or 3 tablespoons dried rosemary, crumbled
4 1/2-by-3-inch strips lemon zest
1 1/4 cups lemon juice (from about 5 lemons)
3 tablespoons Grand Marnier or other orange liqueur

In a medium saucepan, combine the water, sugar, rosemary, and lemon zest. Bring to a simmer, stirring occasionally. Remove from the heat, cover, and let infuse for 10 minutes.

In a large glass or stainless-steel bowl, combine the lemon juice and Grand Marnier. Strain the rosemary syrup into the lemon juice and stir to combine. Chill in the refrigerator or, to hasten the process, pour the lemon mixture into a stainless-steel bowl, set it in a larger bowl filled with ice, and stir until cold.

Pour the chilled lemon mixture into two 9-by-9-inch stainless-steel pans. Freeze for 15 minutes. Stir well and return the pans to the freezer. Continue freezing, stirring every 15 minutes, until the granita is completely frozen, about 1 hour in all. When ready to serve, scoop the granita into chilled bowls or stemmed glasses.

Lemon Ice in Lemon Cups

By serving this simple lemon ice in actual lemon cups, it is attractive enough to serve to company.
This light, refreshing dessert is perfect finish after a full meal on a hot summer day.

4 large lemons
1 envelope unflavored gelatin
1 cup sugar

Garnish
Mint leaves & fresh berries

Cut off one third from the top of each lemon, cutting lengthwise. Grate the peel from the cut off sections, saving one half for garnish. Finely chop the rest and set aside. Squeeze 3/4 cup of lemon juice from the lemons. Remove the remaining pulp and membranes from the lemon cups. Cut off a small sliver off the bottom so the cup will stand on it's own, and refrigerate the cups until you are ready to assemble.

In a pot, add the lemon juice, sugar, gelatin, chopped lemon zest and 2 cups of water. Let sit 10 minutes. Turn on the heat and cook just until the sugar and gelatin are completely dissolved. Pour into a 9 inch baking pan and freeze two hours. Remove the lemon mixture from the pan into a mixing bowl. Using an electric mixer, beat until light and smooth, but still frozen. Return the mixture to the baking pan, and freeze until partially frozen, about 2 more hours. Remove from the pan, and beat again as before. Return to the freezer and freeze until firm. Fill the lemon cups with the mixture, and garnish with the remaining grated lemon, mint leaves and fresh berries. Serve immediately.

This is a great recipe to prepare ahead. Just fill the lemon cups, wrap carefully in plastic wrap and freeze until you are ready to serve. Enjoy!

Passion Fruit Granita with Tropical Compote

Frozen passion fruit juice concentrate makes this dessert a snap. Experiment with other frozen concentrates such as pineapple, guava, mango, etc.

One 11.5-ounce can Welch's frozen passion fruit flavor juice cocktail concentrate, thawed
1 1/2 cups water
2 tablespoons fresh lime juice

1/4 small ripe pineapple, peeled, diced
1 mango, peeled, pitted, diced
3 kiwis, peeled, diced
1 tablespoon sugar
1 teaspoon grated orange peel
1 to 2 tablespoons minced crystallized ginger

6 fresh mint sprigs (optional)

Whisk frozen concentrate, water and lime juice in 8- or 9-inch 9metal baking pan until concentrate has thawed. Freeze mixture until icy at edge of pan, about 1 hour, depending on type of freezer. Whisk to distribute frozen portions evenly. Freeze again until icy at edge of pan and overall texture is slushy, about 1 hour. Whisk to distribute frozen portions evenly. Freeze without whisking until solid, about 4 hours. Using fork, scrape granita forming icy flakes.

TIP: Can be made 1 day ahead. Cover with foil and keep frozen. Mix pineapple, mango, kiwi, sugar and orange in medium bowl to blend. Toss with 1 to 2 tablespoons ginger. (Can be made 3 hours ahead. Cover and refrigerate). Spoon granita into 6 frozen Martini glasses, mounding slightly on 1 side. Spoon compote on other side. Garnish with mint, if desired and serve immediately.

Melon Sorbet

Italy's first melons came to ancient Rome from Persia. They were soon being cultivated successfully near the city, in the town of Cantalupo, which gave its name to today's best-known melon variety, showcased here in a light and refreshing sorbet. For the freshest flavor and best consistency, make the sorbet no more than one day in advance of serving.

1/4 cup (2 fl oz/60 ml) water
1/4 cup (2 oz/60 g) plus 1 teaspoon sugar
2 1/2 pounds (1.25 kg) cantaloupes
2 extra-large egg whites

In a deep saucepan, combine the water and the 1/4 cup (2 oz/60 g) sugar and bring to a boil over high heat. Do not stir or the mixture will crystallize. Continue to boil until it becomes a thick and clear syrup, about 5 minutes. Remove from the heat and let cool. Cut the cantaloupes in half, then remove and discard the seeds. Cut off and discard the rind. Chop the pulp coarsely. You should have about 1 1/2 lb (750 g) pulp. Working in batches if necessary, place the melon pulp in a food processor fitted with the metal blade or in a blender and purée until smooth. Transfer the puréed melon to a bowl, add the cooled syrup and stir until blended. Cover and chill well, at least 2 hours.

Transfer the melon mixture to an ice cream maker and freeze according to the manufacturer's instructions. Meanwhile, using a clean bowl and an electric mixer set at high speed, beat the egg whites until frothy. Add the 1 teaspoon sugar and continue to beat until semisoft peaks form. When the melon mixture is slushy and a little frozen, add the egg whites to the mixture and then continue to freeze until solid.

Mocha Semifeddo

A light, creamy, frozen treat that is wonderful after any meal, yet elegant enough to serve guests. Simply remove it from the freezer just before serving, garnish and serve.

Semifreddo

4 large eggs
1/2 cup sugar
1/4 cup water
1/8 teaspoon cinnamon
3/4 cup heavy cream
1/4 cup powdered sugar
2 tablespoons cocoa
1 cup chocolate wafer crumbs
1 tablespoon instant espresso powder dissolved in 1 teaspoon warm water

To Finish

chocolate sauce, warmed (homemade or purchased)
chocolate covered espresso beans
1/2 cup heavy cream whipped with 1/8 cup powdered sugar
cocoa for dusting
edible flowers (optional)

For the semifreddo, begin by lining a 9 x 5 inch loaf pan with plastic wrap, leaving a 2 inch overhang all around. Put the pan in the freezer to cool.

Combine the water and sugar in a small pan over medium heat until the sugar is completely dissolved. While the sugar syrup is heating, beat the eggs in a bowl on medium high speed for about 3-4 minutes or until they are thick and pale. Continue to beat, and slowly add the hot syrup in a small stream. Continue beating until the mixture has doubled in volume and is cool.

Stir in the cinnamon, and sift the cocoa over the bowl, mixing it in evenly.

Whip the cream with the 1/4 cup of powdered sugar until it is almost stiff. Fold this mixture into the beaten eggs and mix well. Pour half of this mixture into the prepared pan, and sprinkle the chocolate cookie crumbs on top being careful not to mix. Return to the freezer for about one hour.

While the first layer is firming up in the freezer, begin preparaing the espresso layer by stirring the dissolved espresso into the remaining mixture. Cover and chill in the refrigerator for the remainder of the hour.

Once the hour is up, gently stir the espresso mixture if it has separated, and carefully pour this mixture on top of the lighter mixture already in the pan. Do not mix! Carefully cover the pan with plastic wrap, and return to the freezer for at least 8 hours, or overnight.

To serve, unmold the semifreddo, and cut into 1 1/2 inch slices. Drizzle a little of the chocolate sauce on each plate, and place the semifreddo slice on top. Put a dollop of whipped cream in the center of the slice, and decorate with a few chocolate espresso beans.

Lightly sift a little cocoa around the plate if desired, and place one edible flower in front of the semifreddo. Serve immediately.

Peach Gelato

Creamy and rich, this gelato recipe makes the most out of sweet, fresh summer peaches. Serve slightly soft as Italian gelato is served.

2 cups, cold fresh peach puree
1 ripe peach, pitted, peeled and chopped into fine dice
2 cups whole milk
2 cups heavy cream
2 egg yolks
1 tablespoon finely chopped lemon zest
1 cup sugar, divided into two

Mix the peach puree with the diced peach and refrigerate until ready to use. Position a sieve or fine strainer over a medium bowl set in an ice water bath. Heat milk, cream, and half the sugar in medium-size heavy saucepan over medium heat, stirring occasionally, until hot, but not boiling. Turn off the heat. Meanwhile, whisk yolks and remaining sugar in medium bowl until pale yellow. Stir half the warmed milk mixture into beaten yolk mixture until just blended. Return this mixture to the saucepan of remaining warmed milk mixture. Heat over medium-low heat, stirring constantly with wooden spoon until steam appears, foam subsides, and mixture just begins to thicken. Do not boil or eggs may curdle. Remove from the heat, and immediately strain the custard into the prepared bowl over ice water. Once the custard has cooled, refrigerate for at least two, or up to 24 hours.

Mix the cold peach puree mixture, and lemon zest into the cold custard and combine thoroughly. Pour this mixture into an ice cream machine canister and churn, following manufacturer's instructions, until the mixture is frozen and semi firm, not hard, which usually takes about 25 to 30 minutes.

Peach Granita

This light, refreshing dessert is perfect finish after a full meal on a hot summer day. Made simply with sweet, ripe peaches and a little sugar syrup, it is a healthy alternative to ice-cream.

Use only ripe peaches for the very best results. You can leave out the raw egg white if you are worried about using raw eggs.

1 cup granulated sugar
1/2 cup water
1 1/2 pound ripe peaches
2 tablespoons fresh lemon juice
1 teaspoon lightly beaten egg white

In a small saucepan, heat the sugar and water until boiling. Stir until the sugar is completely dissolved. Cool the sugar syrup to room temperature.

Peel and pit the peaches and cut into coarse dice. Once you have completed cutting all of the peaches, place them in a food processor and puree until smooth. Measure out two cups of the smooth peach mixture, and reserve the rest for something else. In a separate bowl, mix together the peach mixture, syrup, and lemon juice. Refrigerate until cold for at least two hours.

Stir into the peach mixture the lightly beaten egg white, and place the mixture in an ice-cream maker. Following manufacturers instructions, process until frozen. Either serve the peach ice immediately, or freeze in an airtight container for up to 6 hours.

Spumone

1-1/2 cups heavy cream
1/2 cup sugar
1/2 cup maraschino cherries, diced
3 tablespoon candied orange peel
1 teaspoon lemon juice
1-1/2 qts. vanilla ice cream, slightly softened
1/2 cup chopped almonds
1/4 teaspoon. almond extract

Whip cream until stiff peaks form. Fold in sugar, cherries, orange peel, and lemon juice.

Place in the refrigerator to harden, about 1 hour.

Combine ice cream with almonds and almond extract.

Line a 1-qt. melon mold or small deep bowl with plastic wrap. Press ice cream to about a 1-inch thickness into the bottom and up the sides of the bowl.

Fill the center with the whipped cream mixture. Cover and freeze for 12 hours.

Unmold onto a serving platter. Cut into slices to serve.

Vanilla Ice Cream with Strawberries and Balsamic Vinegar

Many small pizzerias lack the facilities for making elaborate desserts. They instead rely on dolci al cucchiaio, or "spoon desserts," that can be prepared quickly with easily available ingredients. In this popular, rich summertime spoon dessert, piquant balsamic vinegar flavors fresh strawberries and ice cream.

1 pint vanilla ice cream
2 1/2 cups strawberries, stems removed, halved lengthwise
1/4 cup balsamic vinegar, or to taste
1 tablespoon sugar
Coarsely ground pepper

Remove the ice cream from the freezer and let stand at room temperature until it is soft enough to stir into the strawberries, 10-15 minutes, depending upon on how cold the freezer is.

Meanwhile, in a bowl large enough to accommodate the ice cream eventually, stir together the strawberries, 1/4 cup balsamic vinegar, sugar and pepper to taste. The vinegar and sugar will mix with the berries' natural juices to create a sauce-like consistency. Taste and add more vinegar if needed.

When the ice cream is soft enough, add it to the berry mixture. Immediately stir together until the berries and ice cream are evenly distributed. Spoon into tall wine glasses and serve at once.

Fruit

Baked Fruit with Crispy Topping

This is an easy dessert you can throw together in minutes using almost any fruit combination found in your refrigerator. Top with ice cream, sweetened whipped cream, or masacarpone cheese.

3 apples, peeled, cored and cut into 1 inch cubes
3 pears, peeled, cored, and cut into 1 inch cubes
4 - 5 cups mixed frozen berries (I used blackberries and raspberries), thawed and drained
1 cup sugar
2 teaspoons lemon juice
2 tablespoons all-purpose flour

Topping

1/2 cup toasted almonds, finely ground
1 cup regular oats
1 1/2 cup all-purpose flour
3/4 cup brown sugar
1 teaspoon cinnamon
dash of salt
1 cup unsalted butter

Preheat the oven to 375 degrees. F. Mix together the fruits, white sugar, lemon juice and flour. Butter an oval gratin dish (3 quart size), and place the fruit evenly in the dish.

In another bowl, add the dry ingredients and mix. Cut the butter into pieces, and add it to the dry ingredients. Begin to rub the butter into the flour mixture until it begins to clump together. You could also complete this step in a food processor, and pulse until it begins to clump together. Sprinkle the topping over the fruit.

Bake for 30 minutes and then reduce the heat to 350 degrees F. Cook an additional 15 to 20 minutes, or until the top is lightly browned and the fruit is bubbling nicely. Let sit for 15 to 20 minutes. Serve with a scoop of ice cream or sweetened whip cream.

Baked Honeyed Figs

When fresh figs are in season, this is a delicious way to prepare them. You can serve these figs over ice cream, alongside a slice of sponge cake, or on their own topped with a little heavy cream and a sprinkling of cinnamon.

12 fresh black figs
1 teaspoon grated orange or lemon zest
1/4 cup fresh orange juice
2 tablespoons honey

Preheat over to 350 F. Remove stems from figs and arrange the figs in ovenproof dish, pressing down lightly to flatten bottoms so that figs will stand upright. Mix the orange zest, juice, and honey together and pour over the figs.

Bake until the figs are tender and the syrup has thickened, about 20 minutes. Cool and serve as desired.

Baked Peaches with Almond Paste

Stuff ripe, juicy peach halves with pureed almond paste and then bake them until tender and golden. Puree the almond mixture ahead of time if you like, but wait until the last minute to cut and stuff the peaches, or they'll turn brown.

4 peaches, halved and pitted
6 ounces almond paste (about 1/2 cup)
3 tablespoons hot water
1 teaspoon lemon juice
1 1/2 teaspoons cold butter, cut into 8 pieces

Heat the oven to 400 degrees F. Put a rack on a baking sheet and then put the peaches on the rack, skin-side down.

In a food processor, puree the almond paste, water, and lemon juice. Spoon the almond mixture into the centers of the peaches. Top each mound of almond paste with a piece of the butter.

Bake in the lower third of the oven until the peaches are tender and the almond paste is golden brown, about 25 minutes. Serve warm.

PEELING THE PEACHES: Peel the peaches or not, as you like. The blush on the skin is pretty, but during taste tests most of us pulled off the peel and pushed it to the side of the plate.

ALMOND PASTE: Almond paste is simply a combination of ground almonds and sugar. It's available in supermarkets, usually in the baking aisle, and comes in both cans and tubes.

Cantaloupe-Essensia Granita with Fresh Fruit Compote

This refreshing dessert is the perfect finale to a summer meal. Offer purchased almond macaroons alongside, if desired.

1 large cantaloupe (about 5 pounds), halved, seeded
1 cup Essensia or other sweet Muscat wine
2/3 cup plus 2 tablespoons sugar
1/3 cup water

1 12-ounce basket strawberries, hulled, cut into 1/4 to 1/3-inch dice
1 large nectarine, pitted, finely diced
1 tablespoon very thinly sliced fresh mint leaves

Almond macaroons (optional)

Cut half of melon into 1-inch pieces (about 4 cups). Puree 4 cups melon pieces in food processor (You should have about 3 cups puree). Transfer puree to large bowl. Add Essensia, 2/3 cup sugar and 1/3 cup water and stir to dissolve sugar. Pour puree into 9-inch metal baking pan. Freeze until partially set, whisking twice, about 2 hours. Freeze uncovered until firm, at least 3 hours or overnight. Run tines of fork across surface of granita, forming icy flakes. Cover scraped granita in pan with foil and freeze until ready to serve. Cut enough remaining melon into 1/4-inch dice to measure 1 cup. Transfer to large bowl. Add strawberries, nectarines, 2 tablespoons sugar and mint and toss to coat. (Can be made 4 hours ahead. Cover and refrigerate.) Spoon some of compote into 6 frozen Martini glasses. Mound granita atop compote. Top with a little more compote. Serve immediately, passing cookies separately, if desired.

Chocolate Dipped Figs

Tender, moist dried figs are stuffed with candied peel and are then dipped in chocolate creating a delicious confection that makes a wonderful addition to a holiday cookie tray, or served on their own after dinner with coffee or sweet wine. There are many variations of stuffed figs, but this is my favorite by far. The only trick is to buy dried figs that are moist and tender, and to use good quality chocolate. I find either dark chocolate or semisweet chocolate works best.

12 moist figs
1/4 cup candied orange peel
1/2 cup dark or semisweet chocolate

Trim the stems off the figs, and with a sharp knife, cut a slit down the center. Insert a piece of the orange into the slit. In a double boiler, or in a small pot set into a larger pot of simmering water, melt the chocolate, stirring frequently. Once the chocolate is melted and smooth, dip the figs into the chocolate coating the bottom only. Place the completed figs on a plate or tray, and refrigerate until the chocolate has set. Store in an airtight container in the refrigerator for up to two weeks.

Figs with Honey and Champagne

1 pound dried Calimyrna figs
1 cup warm water
1 1/2 cups of vanilla
1 tablespoon honey
2 teaspoons sugar
3 long strips lemon zest
3 bay leaves
1/2 teaspoon fennel seeds, lightly toasted

In a medium saucepan, combine the figs and water and let stand for 1 hour. Add the wine, honey, sugar, lemon zest and bay leaves and bring to a boil. Reduce the heat to low and simmer the figs until softened, about 20 minutes.

With a slotted spoon, transfer the figs to a bowl. Boil the cooking liquid until syrupy, 6 to 8 minutes. Remove the strips of lemon zest and the bay leaves and pour the syrup over the figs. Sprinkle with the fennel seeds and serve warm.

WINE RECOMMENDATION:

Italians match the sweetness of their desserts with light, and slightly sweet, Muscat-based wines to add a grace note to the finale of the meal. Try a Moscato d'Asti, such as the 1997 Vietti Cascinetta or the 1996 Bera.

Fried Strawberries

This is a unique way to serve strawberries that is absolutely delicious. Make sure your berries are very fresh and ripe for the best results.

1 pound strawberries, cleaned
1/2 cup sugar
1/2 cup sweet liqueur, such as Maraschino
1/3 cup all-purpose flour
1 egg
1 egg white
2 tablespoons unsalted butter, softened
milk
1/4 cup brandy
oil for frying
powdered sugar

Mix the sugar with the liqueur, and add the berries. Mix well, and let sit for about one hour. In a bowl, mix together the flour and butter. Add the egg, and brandy. Add enough milk to make a smooth batter. Beat the egg white until stiff, and then fold this into the batter. Heat the oil to 375 degrees F. Dip the berries into the batter, and fry until golden. Drain on paper towels, sprinkle with powdered sugar, and serve.

Grilled Pineapple

Grilling does wonderful things to fruit as it caramelizes the sugars creating a golden brown color and intensity of flavor. All you need to add is a little ice cream, a few chopped nuts, and you will have a dessert your family will ask for time after time. This is a nice, light summer time dessert to enjoy after a long hot day.

1 large fresh pineapple, peeled, cored and cut into 8 slices
tablespoons melted butter
1/4 cup of liqueur of choice, or maple syrup
vanilla ice cream
toasted coarsely chopped nuts

Brush the pineapple slices with the melted butter and grill until they are tender and golden brown, around 4 minutes on each side. During the last minute of cooking brush with the liqueur or maple syrup. Remove from the heat and cut into bite sized pieces. In individual bowls, divide the pineapple pieces, top with a scoop of vanilla ice cream, and sprinkle on the toasted nuts. You can add an additional drizzle of the liqueur or syrup over the ice cream if you choose.

Honey-Baked Figs with Ice Cream

Use purplish-black Mission figs, green-skinned Calimyrnas, or both for this great-tasting dessert. Give the figs a gentle squeeze to check for ripeness; they should be quite soft.

12 fresh figs
1 1/2 teaspoons olive oil
4 teaspoons honey
2 tablespoons cold butter, cut into 12 pieces
2 tablespoons water
1 pint vanilla ice cream

Heat the oven to 425 degrees F. Cut the stems off the figs. Rub the oil over the figs and put them in a baking pan, stem-side up. Cut a cross in the top of each fig, cutting almost to the bottom.

Drizzle the honey over the figs. Top each one with a piece of the butter. Bake the figs until they open up like flowers, 8 to 10 minutes. Remove the pan from the oven.

Put the figs on plates, add the water to the pan, return the pan to the oven for 1 minute, and then stir to make a sauce. Drizzle the sauce over the warm figs and serve with a scoop of vanilla ice cream on the side.

VARIATIONS:

Sprinkle one-half cup chopped walnuts or pistachios over the figs after the first seven minutes of cooking.

Mangoes and Strawberries in Sweet White Wine

Mangoes are not native to Italy, and absolute fidelity to indigenous ingredients would suggest you do this dish with peaches. If you can buy peaches that were picked ripe and are succulently sweet, forget the mangoes. I never see such peaches, except for a week or two in August, so for the rest of the year mangoes, their exotic flavor and texture notwithstanding are a more desirable choice. If they are still firm, let them ripen for 2 to 4 days at room temperature, until they begin to give under light pressure from your thumb.

2 small, ripe mangoes or 1 large one or peaches
1 1/2 cups fresh strawberries
2 tablespoons granulated sugar
The peel of 1 lemon grated without digging into the white pith beneath
1 cup good sweet wine (see note below)

Peel the mangoes (or the peaches) and slice the flesh off the pits. If using peaches, split them in half and remove the pit. Cut the fruit into bite-size pieces of about 1 inch, and put them in a serving bowl.

Wash the strawberries in cold water, remove the stems and leaves, and slice them lengthwise in half, unless they happen to be very small. Add them to the bowl.

Add the sugar, lemon peel, and wine to the bowl, and toss the fruit thoroughly, but gently to avoid bruising it. Refrigerate and let steep for 1 to 2 hours. Serve chilled, tossing the fruit once or twice before bringing it to the table.

NOTE: The ideal wine for macerating fruit is one made from moscato, the most aromatic of all grapes. Throughout the Italian peninsula, and beyond it to the Sicilian Islands, ravishing sweet muscat wines are made, and if you chance upon one of these, do not pass it by. If you are obliged to choose a substitute, any fine, natural, late-harvest sweet white wine from Germany, South Africa or California will do.

134

Peaches Poached in Wine

One of the wonders of summer, peaches are showcased in this easy dessert. The amount of sugar added to the poaching liquid will depend upon the wine's relative dryness; the liquid should be just sweet enough to heighten the natural sweetness of the peaches. To dress up the dish, top each serving with a dollop of mascarpone.

6 yellow- or white-fleshed peaches
1 bottle fruity white wine or red wine or Champagne
1/3-2/3 cup sugar
1 vanilla bean, split lengthwise

Bring a saucepan three-fourths full of water to a boil. One at a time, dip each peach into the boiling water for 5 seconds. Lift out with a slotted spoon and, using a sharp paring knife, peel the peaches. Halve each fruit along the natural line and remove the pits.

In a saucepan large enough to hold all the peaches in a single layer, combine the wine, 1/3 cup sugar and vanilla bean. Place over low heat and stir until the sugar dissolves. Taste and add more sugar as needed to achieve a pleasant sweetness. Bring to a simmer, add the peaches and simmer until barely tender, 2-5 minutes, depending upon their ripeness.

Transfer the peaches and their cooking liquid to a deep glass bowl (the peaches should be completely covered by the liquid) and let cool to room temperature. Cover tightly with plastic wrap and refrigerate for at least 2 days or for up to 3 days.

TO SERVE: Using a slotted spoon, transfer the peach halves to large wineglasses, placing 2 halves in each glass. Half-fill each glass with the poaching liquid and serve.

135

Poached Autumn Pears with Mascarpone and Ginger

In Italy, autumn's choicest pears are often poached with sugar in a dry white or red wine. This recipe departs from convention, cooking them instead in a naturally sweet dessert wine. One of the best wines to use is Moscato d'Asti from Piedmont, which is made in both sparkling and still forms, and becomes a delicious honeylike syrup when reduced. If unavailable, any light, fruity dessert wine would do nicely.

For Pears

2 large ripe pears
1 1/2 cups Moscato d'Asti wine
1 stick cinnamon, 3 inches long, broken in half
1/2 teaspoon allspice berries or 1 whole clove

For Topping

1/2 cup mascarpone cheese
2 teaspoons confectioners' sugar, or to taste
1 teaspoon milk
2 teaspoons chopped candied ginger
4 fresh mint sprigs, optional
FOR PEARS: Cut the pears in half lengthwise, then core and peel the halves. In a saucepan, combine the wine, cinnamon and allspice berries or the clove and bring to a boil.

Place the pears in the liquid, cored side down, reduce the heat to medium-low and simmer for 4-5 minutes. Turn the pears over and poach until barely soft when pierced with a sharp knife, 4-5 minutes longer. Using a slotted spoon, carefully place each pear half, cored side down, in the center of an individual plate.

Reduce the poaching liquid over medium heat until it forms a thick syrup, about 5 minutes. Strain through a fine-mesh sieve into a clean container. Discard the contents of the sieve.

136

FOR TOPPING: In a small bowl, whisk together the mascarpone, sugar and milk until smooth.

TO SERVE: Cut each pear half into a fan shape: Hold a paring knife at a 45-degree angle to the pear, and make slashes completely through it, but leave the top intact. Gently press on the slices to spread them out, and then drizzle the reduced syrup over the top. Put a dollop of the mascarpone mixture at the top of each pear. Sprinkle evenly with the candied ginger and garnish with the mint sprigs, if desired.

Stuffed Baked Pears

Tender baked pears are stuffed with an amaretti cookie filling, topped with vanilla ice cream and drizzled with chocolate sauce in this elegant recipe. Chocolate and pears are a great combination. This dish is very nice for entertaining as it can be prepared ahead, and quickly assembled at the last moment. You can use almond biscotti in place of the Amaretti if you desire.

4 large ripe pears
3/4 cup of Amaretti di Saronno cookies made into crumbs
4 tablespoons softened butter
1 cup white wine
1/2 cup sugar
2 ounces dark chocolate
2-3 tablespoons cream
vanilla ice cream
toasted slivered almonds

Preheat the oven to 375 degrees F. Peel, half and core the pears. Mix together the cookie crumbs with the butter, adding a few tablespoons of the white wine to moisten. Stuff the cored centers of the pears and set them in a baking dish. In a saucepan, heat together the sugar and white wine until the sugar has completely melted. Pour this mixture into the bottom of the baking dish and place in the oven. Bake for about 35-45 minutes or until the pears are fork tender, spooning the wine sauce over the pears occasionally while they cook. Be careful not to over saturate the filling. Remove from the oven and either serve warm or at room temperature.

Prepare the chocolate sauce by melting the chocolate with the cream over medium heat. To assemble your dish, place each stuffed pear in an attractive goblet, and spoon over it a tablespoon or two of the wine syrup. Place on top of this one small scoop of vanilla ice cream. Next drizzle with your prepared chocolate syrup, sprinkle with the almonds and serve.

138

Sweet Gorgonzola with Baked Figs and Honey

Serving cheese as dessert, or just preceding dessert, is a European tradition. Here, the rich flavors of the cheese and the baked figs are offset by an extraordinary balance of sweet honey and the peppery nature of arugula. Select a sweet, not salty, cheese at its peak of ripeness. Offer thinly sliced walnut bread on the side and accompany with a sweet wine such as a Moscato or Malvasia.

4 firm yet ripe figs
1 1/2 teaspoons extra-virgin olive
10 oz sweet Gorgonzola cheese, rind removed and cut into 4 equal pieces
4 tablespoons acacia or wildflower honey
12 arugula sprigs

Preheat an oven to 475 degrees F. Snip off the pointed tips of the figs and brush the fruits with the olive oil. Arrange in a small baking pan. Place in the center of the oven and immediately reduce the heat to 425 degrees F. Bake until puffed and aromatic, about 10 minutes. Remove from the oven and let cool.

Cut an X in the top of each fig and fold the corners back to resemble a flower, or split in half lengthwise. On each plate, attractively arrange 1 piece Gorgonzola, 1 fig and 3 arugula sprigs and drizzle with 1 tablespoon honey. Serve immediately.

Tuscan Meringue with Mixed Berries

Crisp, sweet meringue cups are a perfect foil for sweet berries and cream in this great spring dessert recipe.

Meringue Shell

5 egg whites
1/4 teaspoon cream of tartar
1 cup granulated sugar
1/4 teaspoon cinnamon

Berries

3 cups mixed fresh berries
2 tablespoons sugar
1 tablespoon balsamic vinegar

Topping

1 (8oz) container whipping cream
1/2 cup powdered sugar
1 tablespoon Grand Marnier

For the meringue, preheat the oven to 250 degrees. Line a baking sheet with parchment paper. In a large bowl, beat the egg whites with the cream of tarter until they are foamy. Begin to add the granulated sugar, a spoonful at a time. Also add the cinnamon. Continue to beat until the meringue is very glossy and forms stiff peaks. You may choose to make one large meringue or individual ones at this point.

To make individual ones, spread about 1/2-cup of the meringue into a 3-inch circle on the parchment paper. Adding a little more of the egg white mixture, and using a spatula, shape a rim around the edges. Continue to make more of the meringue shells, spacing evenly across the baking sheet. To make one larger shell, make in the same manner. Bake for about 1-1/2 hours or until firm to the touch. Turn off the oven, but leave the meringue shells in the warm oven for another hour. Cool completely.

To make the berries, mix the cleaned berries with the vinegar and sugar and let sit for at least 2 hours. Prepare the cream by whipping with the sugar until firm peaks form. Fold in the Grand Marnier, and refrigerate.

To assemble, plate an individual meringue on each plate, top with some of the berry mixture, and add a dollop of whipped cream. Use a little extra cinnamon to decorate.

The trick to making this dessert successful is ensuring the meringue shells are very, very dry.

Puddings and Creams

Amaretti Cream

1 tablespoon powdered unflavored gelatin
4 tablespoon water
7 tablespoon sugar
2 cups heavy cream, divided
4 tablespoon Amaretto
4-5 Amaretti cookies

Sprinkle the gelatin over 4 Tb. water and allow to soften about 15 minutes.

In a saucepan, melt the sugar over low heat until caramel color, about 5 minutes. Remove from heat.

In another saucepan, heat 1 cup cream to just a simmer. Gradually stir the hot cream into the caramel sugar.

Add the amaretto and gelatin. Allow to cool to room temperature. Whip 1 cup of remaining cream until stiff. Gently fold it into the caramel mixture.

Spoon the mixture into 6 custard cups and refrigerate about 3 hours.

Crumble the Amaretti cookies in a food processor.

Sprinkle the top of the custard with the crumbs and serve.

Caramel Panna Cotta

This version goes beyond the usual vanilla and is easier because it's not un-molded. For some extra pizzazz, pile diced fresh bananas onto each pudding and drizzle with a little extra caramel.

1 1/2 cups sugar
1 cup water
1 tablespoon light corn syrup
1/3 cup whole milk
2 teaspoons unflavored gelatin
2 1/4 cups heavy whipping cream
Large pinch of coarse (kosher) salt
1 teaspoon vanilla extract

Combine sugar, 1/2 cup water and corn syrup in heavy medium saucepan. Stir over medium-low heat until sugar dissolves, brushing down any undissolved sugar crystals from sides of pan with wet pastry brush. Increase heat and boil without stirring until syrup is deep amber color, continuing to brush down sides of pan occasionally with wet pastry brush and swirling pan for even coloring, about 10 to 11 minutes. Turn off heat. Add remaining 1/2 cup water (mixture will bubble up vigorously).

Using clean wooden spoon, stir caramel until smooth. If necessary, set pan over very low heat and stir until any hard caramel bits dissolve. Pour caramel into small bowl. Cool caramel, cover and let stand at room temperature up to 3 days (caramel will thicken slightly). Place milk in small ramekin; sprinkle gelatin over. Let stand until gelatin softens, at least 15 minutes. Stir whipping cream, 2/3 cup caramel and salt in heavy medium saucepan over medium-high heat until caramel dissolves and mixture comes to simmer. Add gelatin mixture; turn off heat. Stir until gelatin dissolves, about 2 minutes. Mix in vanilla. Pour into large bowl and refrigerate until cool, stirring every 5 minutes, about 40 minutes. Divide among 6 wine goblets. Cover; refrigerate at least 6 hours and up to 2 days.

Caramelized Rice Pudding

Rice pudding is considered a homey treat in Italy, particularly in the north where it is made with the locally grown short-grained Arborio rice. This high-quality rice, generally used for making risotto, results in an especially creamy pudding. The caramelized topping adds a sweet crunch.

3 tablespoons dark rum
1 tablespoon water
1/3 cup raisins
1/2 cup Arborio rice
2 1/2 cups half and half, or more if needed
1/2 vanilla bean, split lengthwise
2 egg yolks
1/2 cup sugar
3/4 cup heavy cream
6 figs, cut in half through the stem end

In a small saucepan, combine the rum and water and bring to a boil. Remove from the heat, stir in the raisins and let stand until needed.

In the top pan of a double boiler, combine the rice, 2 1/2 cups half-and-half and vanilla bean. Bring water in the lower pan to a gentle boil; place the top pan over it (the pan should not touch the water). Cover and cook until the liquid is absorbed and the rice is tender, about 1 hour. Check the level of the liquid occasionally to make sure the pan does not go dry. If the rice is still a bit tough and all the liquid has been absorbed, add a little more half-and-half and cook until the rice softens. The rice mixture should be very thick.

Remove the top pan, uncover and set aside to cool for 5 minutes. Combine the yolks and 1/4 cup of the sugar in a small bowl and whisk to blend. Whisk in a small amount of the rice mixture to warm the yolk mixture slightly, then whisk the yolk mixture into the rice mixture.

Reposition the top pan over the lower pan of gently simmering water and cook uncovered, stirring occasionally, until thickened, 3-4 minutes. Remove the top pan and transfer the contents to a bowl. Cover with plastic wrap pressed directly onto the surface of the rice to prevent a skin from forming. Refrigerate until completely chilled. (The rice can be prepared to this stage up to 1 day before serving.)

In a bowl, whip the heavy cream until stiff peaks form. Remove and discard the vanilla bean from the rice pudding. Drain the raisins. Using a rubber spatula, fold the cream and the raisins into the rice mixture, distributing the raisins evenly and folding only until no white drifts of cream remain. Pack the pudding firmly into six 1/2-cup flameproof ramekins. Level the surface, cover and refrigerate until well chilled before serving.

TO SERVE: Preheat a broiler. Place the ramekins on a baking sheet. Divide the remaining 1/4 cup sugar evenly among the ramekins, sprinkling 2 teaspoons of it evenly over the surface of each pudding. Place the ramekins in the broiler about 2 inches from the heat and broil until the sugar caramelizes, 2-3 minutes. Rotate the ramekins as needed so they brown evenly. Serve immediately, accompanied with the figs.

Chilled Hazelnut Pudding with Honey Zabaglione

For Pudding

2 eggs, separated
2/3 cup superfine sugar mixed with 1/2 tablespoon vanilla extract
8 oz hazelnuts, shelled and processed to a pulp
1 oz hazelnuts, shelled and chopped
1/3 cup heavy cream

For Honey Zabaglione

3 tablespoons liquid honey
1 egg yolk
2 tablespoons brandy
1/3 cup heavy cream, whipped
3 tablespoons shaved white chocolate

For Sauce

1/4 cup sugar
3 oz semisweet chocolate
1/3 cup heavy cream

FOR PUDDING: Mix the hazelnut pulp with 1 egg white then add the chopped hazelnuts (reserving some for garnish), 2 egg yolks, vanilla sugar and cream.

Fill 4 individual molds with the mixture. Refrigerate for a few hours.

FOR SAUCE: Dissolve the sugar in the water in a saucepan. Add the chocolate and stir to melt. Set aside to cool. Whip cream. Fold into the chocolate mixture.

FOR HONEY ZABAGLIONE: Beat the honey with the egg yolk and brandy in a double boiler over simmering water for about 10 minutes - it should be a dense creamy consistency. Remove from the heat. Fold in the whipped cream.

Chocolate and Coffee Pudding

No one seems to know why this very old and much loved dessert is called a Belgian pudding. It has been cooked in the kitchens of ancient aristocratic families in Mantua for centuries and is so special that no one is willing to part with the recipe.

To make the dessert, you will need a 2-inch-deep 10-inch-diameter tube pan or savarin mold that has a hole in the center and a capacity of 11 or 12 cups. I recommend one with a nonstick surface because it is so easy to unmold. Do not substitute an angel food cake pan. Use instant espresso powder, not finely ground espresso coffee.

3 1/2 ounces semi sweet chocolate
1 quart heavy cream
1/2 cup sugar
1 tablespoon powdered instant espresso coffee
4 large eggs, beaten well

For Caramel
1 cup sugar
4 tablespoons water

Preheat the oven to 350 degrees.

Shave the chocolate into flakes and set it in a 2-quart heavy-bottomed saucepan. Add the cream, sugar, and powdered coffee, set over very low heat, and melt the chocolate, stirring from time to time. Be very careful that the mixture doesn't boil. Once the chocolate has melted, set the mixture aside to cool to room temperature. Add the beaten eggs to the cooled chocolate mixture.

Caramelize the sugar by combining the sugar and water in a small heavy saucepan. Mix well over medium heat with a metal spoon only, then wipe down any crystals of sugar from the side of the pot with a brush dipped in cold water. Bring to a boil and cook without stirring until the mixture is a deep amber color and has caramelized, about 5 to 7 minutes.

148

You will have to work very fast: pour immediately to coat both the sides and bottom of a 10-inch tube pan or savarin mold with an 11- or 12-cup capacity. Set aside to cool.

Place the filled tube pan in a baking pan, pour in simmering water to reach halfway up the sides of the tube pan, and cover the top of the baking pan with foil. Bake for about 1 hour and 10 minutes to 1 hour and 20 minutes, until the chocolate-colored top is set and a skewer comes out clean. If the pudding jiggles a bit, don't worry; it will become slightly firmer as it cools. Cool to room temperature, then cover with plastic wrap and refrigerate. To unmold, dip the mold very briefly in hot water. Loosen the top of the dessert by inserting the tip of a sharp paring knife between the pudding and the mold, about 1/4 inch below the top of the pudding, and drawing it all around the interior of the mold. Place a platter on the dessert and invert to serve.

Crème Brulee

Although this is essentially an extremely easy recipe, there is no better way to end a meal than with this tasty recipe.

This traditional dessert is actually French in origin, but can now be found across Italy. The crisp sugar topping can be made with either a kitchen torch, or the oven broiler.

1 cup heavy cream
2/3 cup milk
7 egg yolks
1/2 vanilla bean (or 1 teaspoon vanilla extract)
1/2 cup sugar, with extra for the topping

Preheat the oven to 250 degrees F. Bring the cream and milk to a boil with the vanilla bean. Remove from the heat, and let cool for 5 minutes. In a bowl, beat together the egg yolks and sugar. Begin to add some of the milk mixture to the bowl, mixing well. Continue until all the milk has been combined with the egg mixture. Pour this mixture through a fine strainer, and into 4 individual ramekin dishes. Place these dishes carefully on a baking sheet, and place in the oven. Bake for about 50 minutes until almost firm. Cool to room temperature, and then refrigerate for at least 2 hours. Sprinkle some additional sugar on top, and either broil or use a kitchen torch to caramelize the sugar.

The surface will crisp up as the sugar cools.

Espresso Flan

A pudding style of dessert that is very similar to the famous Crème Caramel, only the custard is coffee flavored instead. This traditional flan can also be found under the name Latte alla Portuguese.

6 eggs (room temperature)
1/2 teaspoon vanilla extract
3 cups milk
3/4 cup sugar
1/2 cup brewed espresso

Beat the eggs with 1/4 cup of the sugar, until light in color and thickened, about 5 minutes. Add the vanilla extract, and mix. Add the espresso and milk, and mix again. Put the remaining sugar in a small saucepan, and add a teaspoon or so of water. Cook over low heat until you have syrup. Increase the heat, and cook until the mixture turns amber brown, about 3 minutes or so later. Pour the caramel mixture into individual ramekins (custard cups), and place the ramekins in a pan large enough to hold them all. Add enough boiling water to come up to the halfway mark on the ramekins. Divide the custard evenly in the cups. Bake at 350 degrees F. for about 50 minutes or until the centers are set. Cool to room temperature, and then refrigerate at least 3 hours before serving. To serve, dip the bottom of the ramekins into very hot water for a minute or two. Turn over and unmold onto individual plates. Serve immediately.

Individual Orzo Puddings

1/2 cup orzo
1/2 cup heavy cream (whipping)
1 1/2 cups milk
1/3 cup superfine sugar
2 teaspoons vanilla extract
2 teaspoons finely grated orange zest
2 whole eggs
1 egg yolk
1 tablespoon orange marmalade
1 tablespoon Grand Marnier liqueur

Cook the orzo in boiling salted water until al dente. Drain and set aside.

Preheat the oven to 350 degrees F.

Combine the cream, milk, sugar, vanilla and orange zest in a saucepan. Stir over low heat, without boiling, until the sugar is dissolved. Add the orzo, bring to a boil, and simmer for 3 minutes. Remove from the heat.

Beat the eggs and egg yolk in a bowl. Gradually beat them into the milk mixture. Divide the resulting custard among six 1/2 cup ramekins. Place the ramekins in a large baking dish. Add enough boiling water to come halfway up the sides of the ramekins. Bake for 1 hour.

Combine the marmalade and Grand Marnier in a small saucepan and warm gently.

Remove the ramekins from the baking dish and brush the tops with the combined jam and liqueur. Serve the puddings warm.

Orange Mousse

Dessert creams have always had a place in Italian cuisine, even in the most ancient recipes. In the early days, however, the cream base was often fried.

For a more elegant presentation of this simple, wonderfully flavored cream, a little gelatin is often added. In this case it should be refrigerated for a few hours until set, and then turned out of its mold and decorated as desired. It is then often accompanied by a very dark chocolate sauce, preferably hot.

4 eggs, separated
2/3 cup superfine sugar
2 tablespoons potato flour
2 tablespoons Grand Marnier
2 cups fresh orange juice
Grated zest of 1 orange

In the top of a double boiler, whisk the egg yolks with the sugar until the mixture falls from the whisk in a flat ribbon shape, onto the rest of the batter.

Set the pan over simmering water and continue beating as you gradually add the other ingredients: the potato flour, Grand Marnier, orange juice and zest. Continue cooking, without boiling, until you have a thick cream. Remove from the heat; let cool slightly.

Beat 2 of the eggwhites until stiff. Fold into the cream. Pour the mousse into a glass dish or goblet and refrigerate until ready to serve.

Pan Forte Recipe

1 1/4 cups (6 ounces) whole unblanched almonds
1 1/2 cups (6 ounces) whole unblanched hazelnuts
1 teaspoon ground cinnamon
3/4 teaspoon ground ginger
1/4 teaspoon ground cloves
1/4 teaspoon freshly grated nutmeg
1 teaspoon freshly ground black pepper
1 cup plus 2 tablespoons unbleached all-purpose flour
1 tablespoon unsweetened cocoa powder, plus extra for dusting
1 1/4 pounds dried fruits, preferably organic - any combination of
black currants, white or black raisins, black mission figs, white
figs, sour cherries, plums, prunes, pears, peaches, nectarines, or
cranberries and apricots and candied ginger
2/3 cup mild-flavored honey, such as clover
1 cup granulated sugar

Place the ring or mold over the sheet of rice paper on parchment-
lined baking sheet. Adjust the oven rack to the middle position
and preheat the oven to 325 degrees F.

Spread the nuts on a baking sheet in two separate piles, and toast
in the oven until lightly browned, about 10 to 15 minutes. Shake
the pans halfway through to ensure that the nuts toast evenly.
Allow to cool a few minutes. Gather the hazelnuts into kitchen
towel and rub them together to remove the skins. Turn the oven
down to 300 degrees F.

In a large bowl, combine the nuts with cinnamon, ginger, cloves,
nutmeg, pepper, flour, and cocoa powder. Cut the fruit into 1/2-
inch pieces and toss with nut mixture.

In a small saucepan, stir together the honey and sugar. Over high
heat, bring to a boil without stirring. Using a pastry brush dipped
in water, brush the sides of the pan to remove any undissolved
sugar granules. Cook until the sugar reaches 224 to 240 degrees F
(soft ball stage) on a candy thermometer.

Remove from the heat and pour into the fruit mixture. Stir to combine as well as possible. The mixture will be very thick and sticky.

Dip your hands in water and press the fruit mixture evenly into the pan. Bake for 1 hour, until the top is slightly puffed and the surface is matte. Remove from the oven and cool completely in the pan. Trim the rice paper around the edge of the mold. Store at room temperature, wrapped tightly in plastic wrap for several weeks.

Panna Cotta

This dessert is a light, tasty and refreshing way to end a meal. You can top it with almost anything, but I have chosen to use a simple strawberries and sugar.

Panna Cotta literally translates as "cooked cream".

2 1/2 cups of milk
2/3 cup of heavy cream
1 teaspoon vanilla extract
1 1/2 envelopes of unflavored gelatin
1/3 cup of sugar

In a saucepan, combine 2 cups of milk and the cream. Heat until simmering. Sprinkle the gelatin over the remaining 1/2 cup of milk. Remove the milk mixture from the heat, and stir in the vanilla and the softened gelatin. Pour into 6 (1/2cup) custard cups and chill at least two hours.

Topping

1 package frozen strawberries, thawed
3/4 cup of sugar (or to desired sweetness)

Blend the berries and sugar together in a food processor, and strain for seeds. Place over medium heat and bring to a boil. Turn down and simmer for 5 minutes. Cool. To serve, gently run a knife around the edge of each custard cup and unmold on a plate. Serve with a drizzle of the strawberries and sugar topping.

Peach Panna Cotta with Blackberry Sauce

1 can peach nectar (such as Kern's)
2 teaspoons unflavored gelatin
2 pounds fresh ripe peaches, peeled, pitted

1 3/4 cups whipping cream
6 tablespoons sugar
1/2 teaspoon vanilla extract

Blackberry-Cassis Sauce
Fresh blackberries, for garnish
Fresh mint sprigs, for garnish

Place 1/4 cup peach nectar in small bowl. Sprinkle gelatin over.
Let stand 10 minutes to soften. Boil remaining nectar in heavy
medium saucepan until reduced to 1/2 cup, about 12 minutes.
Chop 1 peach and transfer to blender. Add reduced nectar and
blend until puree is completely smooth.

Heat cream and sugar in same heavy medium saucepan over
medium heat, stirring to dissolve sugar. Remove from heat. Whisk
in gelatin mixture. Transfer cream mixture to medium bowl. Stir
in peach puree and vanilla. Ladle into 8 lightly oiled 3 1/4 x 2 1/2 x
1 3/8-inch oval ceramic molds. Refrigerate uncovered until set, at
least 1 day.

DO-AHEAD TIP: Panna cotta can be made up to 3 days ahead.
Cover and keep refrigerated.

Slice remaining peaches. Run small sharp knife around each mold.
Dip mold into bowl of hot water for 3-4 seconds. Invert each
custard into center of large shallow bowl. Arrange sliced peach
around custards. Spoon Blackberry-Cassis Sauce over. Garnish
with fresh blackberries and mint and serve.

Poppy Seed Pudding

Poppy seeds are a distinguishing feature of the cuisine of Upper Adige. In some areas - the Val Senales, for example - children are given big sweet fritters filled with poppy seeds and chestnut jam for afternoon tea. This pudding is from the Val d'Ultimo in the mountains behind the Stelvio massif, on the border with the Valtellina. Vatellina is Italy's major buckwheat-producing area.

1 cup milk
3 tablespoons sugar
7 tablespoons butter, softened
1 1/4 cups buckwheat flour
4 eggs, separated
3 tablespoons poppy seeds, ground

Preheat the oven to 350 degrees F. Place the milk and sugar in a saucepan and bring to a boil. Beat the butter and add the flour. Off the heat, add to the milk and mix well.

Beat the egg yolks with the poppy seeds. Beat the egg whites until stiff.

Stir the egg yolk mixture into the milk mixture.

Pour the mixture into 4 individual molds. Set the molds in a roasting pan and add hot water to reach halfway up the sides. Bake in the oven for 30 minutes until the puddings are evenly browned. Chill and serve.

Quick Cannoli Pudding

15 ounces part-skim ricotta cheese

3 tablespoons sugar

1 tablespoon orange juice

1-1/2 tsp. grated orange peel

1/4 cup mini-chocolate chips

In a medium bowl, stir together the ricotta, sugar, orange juice, and zest until well combined. Fold in the chocolate chips.

Serve at room temperature or chilled.

Rice Pudding

3 cups milk
3/4 cup rice
3 cups half and half
3 eggs
3/4 cup sugar
1 teaspoon vanilla
1/2 cup currants
cinnamon for dusting

In a saucepan over medium heat, bring milk to a simmer.
Add rice, stir, cover and simmer 30 minutes or until milk is
absorbed. Remove from heat.

Stir in half and half and sugar.

In a small bowl, whisk the eggs, and then stir into the rice
mixture.
Return the saucepan to medium heat and stir until the mixture
thickens, about 5 minutes.

Remove from heat. Stir in vanilla and currants.

Pour into a serving dish and sprinkle with cinnamon.

Chill 3-4 hours before serving.

Sour Cream Panna Cotta with Vanilla and Red Wine-Infused Strawberries

A simple and delicious dessert.

Tip: Hulling two pounds of strawberries can be a tedious task. But it's not a chore when using a strawberry huller - a smart tool that makes easy prep work of this task, snipping the stems off effortlessly.

1 cup whole milk
1 1/2 teaspoons unflavored gelatin
1/3 cup plus 1/4 cup sugar
1 cup whipping cream
1 cup sour cream
1 vanilla bean, halved lengthwise then crosswise
2 pounds strawberries, hulled, sliced
1/2 cup fruity red wine, such as Merlot

Pour milk into heavy medium saucepan. Sprinkle gelatin over milk. Let stand until gelatin softens, about 10 minutes. Bring milk mixture to simmer, stirring until gelatin dissolves. Remove from heat. Stir in 1/3 cup sugar. Gradually stir in whipping cream. Whisk in sour cream. Scrape seeds from half of vanilla bean into sour cream mixture; mix well (reserve pod). Pour mixture into six ½-cup ramekins or soufflé dishes. Refrigerate until set, about 4 hours. Combine strawberries, wine and remaining 1/4 cup sugar in medium bowl. Scrape in seeds from remaining half of vanilla bean; add pod. Stir to combine. Cover and let stand until very juicy, about 4 hours.

Tip: Panna cotta can be prepared 3 days ahead. Cover with plastic and keep refrigerated. Strawberries can be prepared 1 day ahead; refrigerate. Invert panna cotta into 6 shallow bowls. Surround with strawberries and juices.

Zabaglione

5 large egg yolks
5 tablespoons granulated sugar
1/4 cup sweet Marsala wine
1/4 cup Grand Marnier or other orange-flavored liqueur
1/2 cup heavy cream
1 1/2 tablespoons confectioners' sugar

TO COOK THE ZABAGLIONE: Set up a double boiler or set a medium-size stainless-steel bowl over a pot of simmering water. Check to make sure the bottom of the bowl is not touching the water, or the eggs may scramble and overcook. Whisk the egg yolks, sugar, Marsala wine and Grand Marnier together and place them in the pot or bowl over the simmering water. Continue to whisk vigorously until the eggs increase in volume and thicken; this should take 2 to 3 minutes. It's important to move the whisk around the bowl so the eggs cook evenly. If the edges of the eggs start to scramble, remove the bowl from over the water and continue to whisk. The final zabaglione should be like an airy pudding.

Whisk the zabaglione over a bowl of ice to cool, and then set aside. Whip the cream over the ice until it stands in soft peaks, then sift in the confectioners' sugar. Fold the whipped cream into the cool zabaglione and refrigerate for 1 to 2 hours. The zabaglione can be prepared a day ahead. Serve it with panettone or pound cake.

4428382

Made in the USA
Lexington, KY
25 January 2010